Cellular Manufacturing:
Integrating Technology and Management

ENGINEERING MANAGEMENT SERIES

Series Editor: **Dr. John A. Brandon**
        University of Wales, Cardiff, UK

Cellular Manufacturing: Integrating Technology and Management

John A. Brandon

Cardiff School of Engineering
University of Wales, Cardiff, UK

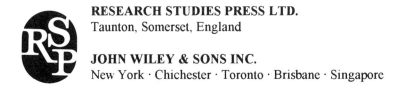

RESEARCH STUDIES PRESS LTD.
Taunton, Somerset, England

JOHN WILEY & SONS INC.
New York · Chichester · Toronto · Brisbane · Singapore

RESEARCH STUDIES PRESS LTD.
24 Belvedere Road, Taunton, Somerset, England TA1 1HD

Marketing and Distribution:
Australia and New Zealand:
Jacaranda Wiley Ltd.
GPO Box 859, Brisbane, Queensland 4001, Australia
Canada:
JOHN WILEY & SONS CANADA LIMITED
22 Worcester Road, Rexdale, Ontario, Canada
Europe, Africa, Middle East and Japan:
JOHN WILEY & SONS LIMITED
Baffins Lane, Chichester, West Sussex, UK, PO19 1UD
North and South America:
JOHN WILEY & SONS INC.
605 Third Avenue, New York, NY 10158, USA
South East Asia:
JOHN WILEY & SONS (SEA) PTE LTD.
37 Jalan Pemimpin 05-04
Block B Union Industrial Building, Singapore 2057

Library of Congress Cataloging-in-Publication Data

Available

Coventry University

British Library Cataloguing in Publication Data
A catalogue record for this book is available from the British Library.

ISBN 0 86380 191 9 (Research Studies Press Ltd.) *[Identifies the book for orders except in America.]*
ISBN 0 471 96143 4 (John Wiley & Sons Inc.) *[Identifies the book for orders in USA.]*

P₆ 6760

Printed in Great Britain by SRP Ltd., Exeter

CONTENTS

PREAMBLE

Hegel says somewhere that all great events and personalities in world
history reappear in one fashion or another. He forgot to add: the first time
as tragedy, the second as farce.

Karl Marx.

This is not a book about technology; neither is it a book about management. The scope
is much narrower, yet as important as either. It is, as its title suggests, about the
integration of management and technology. Of course, this can only be achieved if the
reader has sufficient awareness of the capability and limitations of technology and the
constraints on managerial effectiveness. Much of this knowledge is available elsewhere
and the chosen approach will be to provide sufficient references in the text. Only where it
is absolutely necessary will detailed descriptions of technological concepts or
management theories be described.

The text calls on an extremely wide range of source material from anthropology to zen.
Its central message is that organisational change in manufacturing systems can only be
achieved if technology and management are integrated, and that this is only possible if it
is recognised that the manufacturing enterprise is closely coupled into a complex set of
political, social and economic systems.

In particular, it is necessary to realise that successful integration of technology and
management is dependent on both corporate culture and external social structures.

Implementation of new technologies demands both management commitment and understanding of the technology. All too often management enthusiasm wanes before sufficient experience has been gained to benefit from the introduction of the new technology, leading to a premature declaration of the failure of the strategy.

The book examines the origins and effects of this mismatch of technological capability and management planning. Case studies are presented that typify incompatibilities in phasing of management expectation and technological capability.

The text by Kirton and Brooks (1994) covers similar ground, but the interpretation of the development of manufacturing and its cultures is quite different.

References

J Kirton and E Brooks, 1994, Cells in industry: Managing teams for profit, McGraw-Hill, Maidenhead England.

NEW LAMPS FOR OLD:
A PERSONAL REFLECTION

In manufacturing systems engineering, in particular, and management, in general, little regard is given to the vast base of knowledge and experience which has been accumulated over the last two hundred and fifty years.

Over and over again, managers tread the same paths as their predecessors, their competitors and - the greatest tragedy of all - their contemporaries in the same organisation. To illustrate this, consider a quality seminar given to senior managers at one of the UK's leading manufacturers in early 1992. The speaker asked the delegates to identify four significant contributors to the development of management who appeared in a recent text by Clutterbuck and Crainer (1990). They were able to identify three of the four, all identified with the Japanese manufacturing success story - which had been rammed down their throats by senior management - but not the fourth, a man who had pioneered techniques of action learning (Revans 1979) in their own company in the 1940s.

How can this be explained? Firstly, the simple pragmatic explanation is that few practising industrial managers have the time to read history books. In accordance with the observation by Karl Marx, they are destined to repeat the tragedies of history but as farce. By the same logic, every project engineer knows the first law of project management, that there is never enough time to plan to do the job once properly but there will be endless time to experiment and tinker once the initial disaster is acknowledged.

A second explanation is the absence of a training culture, attributed by Drucker (1971) as the discriminator between the industrial engineer in Japan and the West. Quoting from an unnamed Japanese *leading industrial engineer* - one might guess Taiichi Ohno:

.... we do exactly the same things that the industrial engineer does in Detroit or Pittsburgh; but it means something different. The American industrial engineer lays out the work for the worker. Our industrial engineers are teachers rather than masters. We try to teach how one improves one's own productivity and the process. What we set up is the foundation; the edifice the worker builds.

One can find fewer excuses for the ignorance of academic commentators. However, as an example central to the theme of the current work will illustrate, the opportunity to benefit from the experience of others has been spurned repeatedly. Group Technology is one of the essential options for consideration when cellular manufacturing systems are proposed. In the UK the potential of Group Technology was recognised at an early stage with a group of active researchers based in Manchester at the College of Technology (now University of Manchester Institute of Science and Technology). Five workers - Burbidge, Edwards, Gombinski, Ranson and Allen - are credited by Schonberger (1990) as leading pioneers of cellular manufacturing. It is surprising, therefore, that a similarly eminent engineer, also a Professor at UMIST, Rosenbrock (1990), should apparently make no recognition of the importance of the contribution of his colleagues in his study of the interaction of human factors with advanced manufacturing technology. Almost all of the leading authors on cellular manufacturing systems have overlooked the earliest implementations such as the work of Flanders (1924) at the Jones and Lamson Machine Company. This paper contains descriptions of implementation of what we would describe today as *Design for Manufacture, Group Technology* and *Just-in-Time*. In contrast to the bulk of American companies, as described by Johnson and Kaplan (1987), Jones and Lamson realised the folly of preoccupation with overhead costing, recognising that the large number of clerical staff that this necessitated added no value to the product.

The second reason for the apparent inability of industrial managers to benefit from the lessons of history is that of lack of communication between managers at different levels in the hierarchy within the enterprise. All too often, those who perceive the need for change are powerless to bring it about. As has been described previously by the author elsewhere (Brandon 1992a,b,c), successful management of change in manufacturing systems demands a confluence of authority, resources, motivation and expertise. All too often the first two prerequisites are concentrated in general management whilst the latter two are held by the technologists.

A third candidate explanation of the inability of manufacturing systems engineers to exploit existing knowledge is the *not invented here* syndrome. In appraising achievements elsewhere, too much emphasis is placed on the differences in context between the experience outside the organisation and too little on the similarities. Perhaps equally common, in the estimation of Prietula and Simon (1989), is the tendency to underrate the capability of in-house management. They suggest that simply to appraise the capability of the workforce gives valuable insights into how the organisation works. In most organisations both of these problems will coexist to restrict the ability of the enterprise to introduce, and indeed to implement, concepts of radical change.

As will be seen, very little of the content of the current volume is new. Considerable reliance will be placed on the recorded experience, analysis and opinions of industrial practitioners, consultants and academic commentators. Wherever insights have been recorded elsewhere these will be either summarised or quoted, rather than simply repackaged as the author's own intellectual contribution - a practice which is now dignified by the term *creative swiping* - most probably due to Tom Peters (1987). Perhaps some of the existing knowledge is presented in an original form, but in general no such claim is, or indeed needs to be, made. It is the author's view that awareness of the tragedies of manufacturing systems engineering may be enough to avoid (at least some) future farces.

REFERENCES

J A Brandon, 1992a, Managing Change in Manufacturing Systems, Productivity Press, Olney, England.
J A Brandon, 1992b (April), Strategic Perspectives for Implementation of FMS, Robotics and CIM, 29th International Machine Tool Design and Research Conference, University of Manchester Institute of Science and Technology, 241-247.
J A Brandon, 1992c, Structural impediments to strategic change in the technological enterprise, Journal of Strategic Change, 1(6), 333-9.
D Clutterbuck and S Crainer, 1990, Makers of management: men and women who changed the business world, Macmillan, London.
P F Drucker, 1971 (March-April), What we can learn from Japanese management, Harvard Business Review, 110-122.

6

R E Flanders, 1924, Design, manufacture and production control of a standard machine, Transactions of the American Society of Mechanical Engineers, 46, 691-738.

H T Johnson and R S Kaplan, 1987, Relevance lost: The rise and fall of management accounting, Harvard Business School Press.

T Peters, 1987, Thriving on Chaos: Handbook for a Management Revolution, Macmillan, London.

M J Prietula and H A Simon, 1989 (January-February), The experts in your midst, Harvard Business Review, 120-124.

R W Revans, 1979, Action Learning, Blond and Briggs, London.

H Rosenbrock, 1990, Machines with a Purpose, Oxford University Press.

R J Schonberger, 1990, Building a chain of customers: linking business functions to create the World Class Company, Hutchinson Business Books, London.

IN A FAR-AWAY COUNTRY

A prophet is not without honour, save in his own country and his own house.
Matthew 13:57

If ever there was a prophet without honour in his own country, it was Edwards Deming.
(Anon. 1993)

One of the remarkable features of the analysis of ideas in industrial management is how often the authoritative contributions are recognised first outside their own culture.

This may be achieved through a number of mechanisms:

> Firstly, many of the significant personalities of management migrated from their native culture. Geographically, there are several prominent innovators, for example Peter Drucker (Austrian) and Elton Mayo (Australian), who left the countries of their birth (Drucker via the UK) before undertaking their most significant work. Elliott Jacques is a Canadian whose most significant work was carried out at the British Tavistock Institute of Human Relations and who latterly has worked from the George Washington University.

> Secondly, a number of key contributors emigrated because they found their ideas did not fit into the prevailing drift of national management culture. In Britain the greatest loss is widely acknowledged to be Reg Revans whose ideas on management training (Revans 1979) are widely admired internationally but who

left his native country in disillusionment at the slow progress of acceptance of his methods.

A third category emigrated after they had achieved intellectual recognition at home without substantial financial rewards. Probably the late E L Trist, of the Tavistock Institute of Human Relations, falls into this category.

The fourth category, epitomised by Edwards Deming and Joseph Juran, found that their ideas were unacceptable in their own culture but were recognised overseas (in their cases particularly in Japan). Both were pioneers of the quality movement who gained their industrial experience with William Shewhart, the originator of many of the most important innovations in statistical process control, in the Western Electric Company, where the research of Elton Mayo was also carried out, in the 1920s and 1930s. It is interesting that Gillespie (1991) does not index Shewhart, Deming or Juran in his studies of the Hawthorne experiments. Wille (1992) notes that his first acquaintance with Juran's text *Management Breakthrough* was when he came across it in a batch of second-hand books. He remarks that it would probably be necessary to visit a national depositary collection to read a copy of Shewhart's text *Economic Control of Quality!*

As will be described, innovations often take place in what appears at first sight to be the most unlikely and unreceptive conditions. Group Technology (*qv*), perhaps the earliest cellular manufacturing system, was developed not in an advanced industrial nation but in the Soviet Union (Grayson 1981) during the late 1940s and early 1950s (Mitrofanov 1966). It is an organisational structure which had been tried in American companies in the 1920s (Flanders 1925) and discarded - for good reasons - but which is now the subject of considerable interest in Western economies (Baer 1985). In Britain, Group Technology received government backing in the 1960s but failed to prosper - so much so that in 1978 John Burbidge - one of its most ardent advocates - was prompted to ask *Whatever Happened to GT?*

The corollary to the belief that innovation often occurs outside traditional industrial organisations is that progress may well be stifled if an enterprise attempts to introduce new ideas into a system with long established patterns of organisation and traditional working practices.

The risk of perpetuation of traditional industrial practices has led corporate strategists to locate innovative manufacturing systems some distance from their traditional plants. In their experiments with lean production, General Motors chose firstly a redundant facility in Fremont, California, for their joint venture with Toyota (NUMMI), and secondly a site in Tennessee for their Saturn project, which sought to apply the learning from NUMMI within a wholly owned plant. In each case the facility was deliberately sited far from their Michigan heartland. (Womack et al 1990).

Similarly when the Japanese auto giants entered the UK in the mid/late 1980s they were careful to locate their plants far from the traditional bases of the motor industry.

Superficially this would appear to vindicate the decisions of the indigenous manufacturers in the 1960s to relocate a substantial proportion of their production to greenfield sites (Ford to Halewood, Triumph to Speke and Vauxhall to Ellesmere Port, all on Merseyside, and Rootes to Linwood in Renfrewshire). On closer scrutiny, however, it should be remembered that these plant location decisions were biased by substantial inducements from the British Government to locate in areas of high unemployment resulting from the rundown of traditional industries - chiefly the docks on Merseyside and shipbuilding in Scotland. Not taken into account were two factors: firstly, the unsuitability of the skills base and, secondly, the traditions of industrial militancy aggravated by the stresses of industrial contraction. Vauxhall had, in fact, preferred to site their new plant alongside the existing facility at Dunstable, Bedfordshire, but their policymaking had been overwhelmed by the attractiveness of the government inducements. The Linwood plant was a financial disaster which led to the collapse of the company. The Triumph factory was a victim of the rationalisation of the tottering monster which was British Leyland, driven together under government pressure by the Labour administration of the late 1960s. Ford and Vauxhall have (eventually) made a success of their Merseyside plants but at enormous cost in management and financial terms. At the time, that great industrial commentator, C. Northcote Parkinson, referred to the *..politician who plunges into business, thumbing his Oxford lecture notes and taking the advice of Hungarian exiles...* (Parkinson 1974).

References

Anon., 1993 (December 24th), Obituary: W Edwards Deming, The Times, 17.

A Baer, 1985 (November), With Group Technology, No One Reinvents the Wheel, Mechanical Engineering 60-69.

J L Burbidge, 1978 (September), Whatever Happened to GT? Management Today, 87-89&193.

R E Flanders, 1925, Design Manufacture and Production Control of a Standard Machine, Transactions of the American Society of Mechanical Engineers, 46, 691-738.

R Gillespie, 1991, Manufacturing Knowledge: A history of the Hawthorne experiments, Cambridge University Press.

T J Grayson, 1981 (July), Group Technology in the USSR: Conditions and Prospects, Chartered Mechanical Engineer, 26-30.

J M Juran, 1964, Managerial Breakthrough, McGraw-Hill, Maidenhead.

S P Mitrofanov, 1966, The Scientific Principles of Group Technolgy, British Library Lending Division (Translation of original Russian text).

C N Parkinson, 1974, Big Business, Weidenfeld and Nicolson, London.

R Revans, 1979, Action Learning, Blond and Briggs, London.

W. Shewhart, 1931, Economic Control of Quality of Manufactured Products, Van Nostrand, New York.

Womack, Jones and Roos, 1990, The machine that changed the world, Rawson Associates, New York.

E Wille, 1992, Quality: Achieving Excellence, Century Business, London.

INNOVATION IN MANUFACTURING SYSTEMS: TIME, PLACE AND CONTEXT

A recurring theme in science fiction is that of time travel. It is rather less prevalent in manufacturing systems management. For a moment, however, imagine how Frederick Taylor would react to current trends in organisation of the manufacturing enterprise if we were able to transport him to a modern manufacturing enterprise. What he would very soon find is that many of the industrial practices he devoted his life to eradicating (Taylor 1947) are currently being advocated by the overwhelming majority of modern management authors, from the charismatics, like Tom Peters (1987), to the pragmatists, like Peter Drucker (1992).

Taylor is most remembered for Scientific Management, and the term **Taylorism** is used emotively to induce prejudice against traditional practices in the management of manufacturing systems. There are grounds for suggesting that Scientific Management and Taylorism cannot, and should not, be used synonymously, but it must also be recognised that the pejorative sense implied in the use of the term Taylorism has inevitably become attached to Scientific Management.

In later sections we shall return to Scientific Management and distinguish it from Taylorism, but for the moment consider the view of the influential management author Harold Leavitt:

> *In so eagerly demolishing Taylorism we may have thrown out some useful parts of the baby with the bath water. We may even be repeating some of the mistakes of Taylorism that we have taken such pains to point out.*
>
> (Leavitt 1962).

Even if Taylor had never developed Scientific Management he would still be an extremely important figure in the field of manufacturing systems. By looking at his technical achievements it is possible to appreciate some of the motivation for Scientific Management.

His principal technological claim to fame was that, with Maunsell White of Bethlehem Steel, he developed a heat-treatment process which extended the usable temperature range of tool steels: High-Speed Steel.

Taylor's first public demonstration of High-Speed Steel illustrates the way in which the new technologies could no longer tolerate the organisational traditions of the nineteenth century. A comparative trial of High-Speed Steel against carbon tool steel proved an embarrassing debacle for the new wonder material even though it had produced impressive results in Taylor's private tests.

The explanation was that the operatives used the speeds and feeds appropriate for carbon steel tools which were wholly inappropriate for the replacement material which only showed its superiority at increased cutting speeds. As a consequence, it proved necessary to impose conformance to charts of speed and feed data under prescribed cutting conditions often in spite of clear conflict with the experience and judgment of the operative. In many respects it is this strong conflict between the requirements of Advanced Manufacturing Technology and craft experience which has lain at the root of much of the industrial strife of the twentieth century.

Taylor's personal odyssey to seek the solutions reflects the essential message of the current work, that any significant technological change demands an appraisal of the organisational environment into which it is to be integrated. Without a receptive infrastructure the probability of success is commonly very small. The outcome of Taylor's analysis of the structure of the technological enterprise was Scientific Management.

The writings of Peter Drucker are deservedly considered to be the most influential of 20th-century works. He summarised the contribution of Taylor:

It is fashionable today to look down on Taylor for his outdated psychology, but Taylor was the first man in history who did not take work for granted, but looked at it and studied it. His approach to work is still the basic foundation. And, although Taylor in his approach to the worker was clearly a man of the nineteenth century, he started out with social rather than engineering or profit objectives. What led Taylor to his work and provided his motivation throughout was first the desire to free the worker from the burden of heavy toil, destructive of body and soul. And then it was the hope to make it possible to give the worker a decent livelihood through increasing the productivity of work.

Drucker (1974)

It is ironic that these are exactly the same motivations which are today used to justify the rejection of Taylorism.

REFERENCES

Drucker, P. F., 1974, Management: Tasks, Responsibilities, Practices, Heinemann, London.
Drucker, P. F., 1992, Managing for the Future, Butterworth-Heinemann, London.
Leavitt, H. J., 1962, Unhuman organizations, Harvard Business Review, vol. 40, 90-98.
Peters, T., 1987, Thriving on Chaos: Handbook for a Management Revolution, Excel, New York.
Taylor, F. W. 1947, Principles of Scientific Management, Harper and Row, New York.

EVOLUTION AND REVOLUTION

Firstly, we will consider the social and economic structure which influenced the development of corporate cultures in Europe up to the time when Taylor became active in the last two decades of the nineteenth century. Initially at least, it is necessary to distinguish this environment from that in which Taylor himself operated, for the simple reason that there was no state of unbroken evolution of industrial culture in the United States.

In Europe, at least, the organisation of manufacturing was based on processes rather than products. Luckily the evidence of this remains, in Anglo-Saxon cultures at least, in the family names which have been passed down from generation to generation.

Take, for example, the military specialisation of the members of the Archer family whose forebears were responsible for the victories in battle at Agincourt and Crecy. Their skill was in launching missiles, however, and not in making them. For this they would have relied on a number of other families: the Bowyer family, whose specialism was in the crafting of bows, were ably assisted by the Stringers; to supply arrows required the combined efforts of the Arrowsmiths, to make the heads, and the Fletchers, to set the flights.

Other examples abound. For example, Mr Carter would be dependent on the services of a large number of specialists including Mr Cartwright, Mr Wheeler, Mr Ostler, Mr Farrier and Mr Smith.

Thus the natural organisational pattern of manufacturing, and indeed the overwhelming majority of other engineering activities, are most commonly based on processes rather than products. This is easily understandable since all humans are different, distinguished by strength, intelligence, manual dexterity etc. Once an individual developed a particular skill then it was natural to pass it on to other members of the family group and, if possible, keep specialist knowledge secret from other families. In time powerful craft guilds developed which shared knowledge between each other but jealously guarded the secrets of their craft.

This organisational pattern has many advantages, not least of which was the Quality Assurance provided by skilful craftsmen, who specialised in a particular process, reinforced by the self-regulatory powers of the craft guilds.

There are several significant disadvantages of process-based manufacturing, however, not least the likelihood that the technical secrets of one craft guild may be essential to technological progress by another group. In the absence of knowledge about the availability of the information elsewhere, this would result in either reinventing the idea or unnecessary delays on the progress of a technology.

In many industries a common pattern of evolution of the manufacturing enterprise can be perceived. To take one of the more simple cases, Lord Sieff (1990) described the foundation of the Desmond family business in Northern Ireland in the late nineteenth century. Mrs Annie Desmond, with thirteen children to support, made a living by distributing cut pieces from the local shirt manufacturer to local girls who would make them up into garments which Mrs Desmond would then return to the manufacturer. In short, her business was as a factor, one who buys and sells on commission. As business built up she invested in a pony and trap and then in sewing machines which she rented to the seamstresses. With further expansion, it proved necessary to provide a building where the operations of the business could be centralised. Only then did it prove necessary for the factor to have a factory. Having reached this stage, it was only a small step to full integration when the company dealt with their retailer customer directly rather than their original client manufacturer.

Similar patterns are evident in a wide number of industries but at different periods and apparently without any recognition that similar problems had been encountered, and solved, before. Chaloner and Musson (1963) described the establishment of loomshops in Bristol in 1339. The Arsenal at Venice was an extremely large industrial enterprise in fourteenth-century Italy with over 3000 craftsmen working on the construction and maintenance of the naval force which enforced Venice's trading fleet (Lane 1973, Gallagher 1980).

There is, however, an important qualitative difference between the textile businesses and the Arsenal. In the first case, the business is based on a narrow skill base, often involving a single industrial process, in this case weaving cloth or making up garments. At the Arsenal the skill base was extremely broad, with the craft groups retaining their autonomy. In such circumstances it was by no means unusual for the craft group to be entirely self-managing and self-regulating, contracting to perform specific work packages for the factor. Even today, in the agricultural industry, crop picking is commonly undertaken on a basis of contracts for work quotas executed between landowners and gangmasters.

Wherever such autonomy has been allowed to perpetuate, the historical record shows that it has been defended vigorously by the craft group concerned. For example the efforts to implement a rationalisation of Britain's docks from the 1950s through to the 1980s were frustrated over and over again by the necessity to negotiate with many separate trade unions each representing a different craft specialisation. Often the craft unions were manifestly defending the indefensible. Equally often the management failed to appreciate how deeply entrenched were the attitudes and that these were consequent on the social structures which had evolved over several generations.

It is too simplistic to attribute such resistance to change to intrinsic conservatism, although that may well play a part. Social patterns may be so deeply ingrained that no straightforward solution to their adaptation to changing circumstances is apparent. Trist and Bamforth (1951) studied the impact of new technology in the mining industry in the period immediately after the Second World War. In particular, they recognised that the lines of authority necessary for the new longwall method of cutting coal were incompatible with the traditional control structure, as Taylor had found some sixty years earlier in the steel industry. It is perhaps surprising to learn, particularly after over a decade of propaganda from the Thatcherite ideologues, that a disproportionate number of Britain's outstanding management thinkers, including E F Schumacher (Small is Beautiful) and Reg Revans (Action Learning), were employed by the British National Coal Board during this period (Clutterbuck and Crainer 1990, Kennedy 1991).

The strength of the craft groups should not be underestimated. Groups with specialist skills were in demand throughout the world. A typical example is the ironmasters of South Wales, the craftsmen trained at the great ironworks of Cyfartha, Dowlais, Pennydarren and Plymouth. The Guests, Crawshays and Homfrays turned Merthyr Tydfil from a village in 1750 to the largest town in Wales by 1800 (Thomas 1977).

The ethnic flow was not one way, however. The rapid expansion in industry in South Wales overwhelmed the resources of the local labour market and attracted workers from all over Europe. Particularly important were the skills in deep mining of the Polish and Italian immigrants whose descendants continue to provide a characteristic contribution to the culture of the region.

The skills of the South Wales ironmasters were in demand wherever iron was made. Until the Russian revolution, the Hughes family still lived in their company town Hughesovska in the Ukraine. With the collapse of the Soviet Union in 1990 the surviving members of the family returned to the Ukraine for the first time since 1917, to be greeted with considerable nostalgia and affection.

In France the lengths to which the foundries were prepared to go to make their immigrant Welsh craftsmen feel at home is attested by Hudson (1976), describing the great industrial centre of Le Creusot:

> *On a hillside overlooking the town is a remarkably un-French group of cottages, built early in the nineteenth century to accommodate Welsh miners and ironworkers, who came over with their families to teach industrial skills to the natives.*

Not surprisingly the contribution of Welsh craftsmen was essential to the development of the steel industry in Pennsylvania in the nineteenth century. Like the stars of the modern football transfer market, the craft specialists were mobile, highly prized and knew their worth.

In many respects the accepted image of the "great melting pot" in the formation of the nationhood of the United States is a romantic idealisation. Even where ethnic groups had little in the way of specialist skills, there was a natural inclination to focus on a single aspect of the overall manufacturing process and work as a group. Thus not only did the steel industry of the USA inherit an organisational structure based on craft demarcation but this was also reinforced along ethnic lines.

How, then, could Frederick Taylor introduce the undoubted benefits of his superior cutting technology into a steel industry organised according to extremely strong craft demarcation principles? Those who had most to gain from the new technology, the factory owners, had no direct control over the workforce. The contractors, the gang leaders who actually employed the shop-floor workers, were entirely responsible for the methods which were used to fulfil their agreed quotas. It is difficult to see how they would have benefited from the introduction of new technology, either financially or managerially (Nelson 1980).

Taylor realised, therefore, that evolutionary change had reached its limits and that the effective implementation of the new technology could only be achieved by radical restructuring of the manufacturing enterprise.

References

W E Chaloner and A E Musson, 1963, Industry and technology, Vista, London.
D Clutterbuck and S Crainer, 1990, Makers of Management, Macmillan, London.
C C Gallagher, 1980 (April), The history of batch production and functional factory layout, Chartered Mechanical Engineer.
K Hudson, 1976, The Archaeology of industry, Bodley Head, London.
C Kennedy, 1991, Guide to the Management Gurus, Business Books, London.
F C Lane, 1973, Venice, John Hopkins, Baltimore.

D Nelson, 1980, Frederick W. Taylor and the rise of Scientific Management, University of Wisconsin Press.

M Sieff, 1990, Management the Marks and Spencer way, Weidenfeld and Nicolson, London.

R Thomas, 1977, South Wales, Bartholomew, Edinburgh.

E L Trist and K W Bamforth, 1951, Some social and psychological consequences of the longwall method of coal-getting, Human Relations, 4 (1) pp6-24 and 37-8, reprinted in D S Pugh, 1971, Organization Theory, Penguin, Harmondsworth, pp345-369.

THE EVOLUTION OF THE ENTERPRISE

With the explosion of recent interest in the structure of the enterprise, it may seem perverse that a paper over twenty years (Greiner 1972) old should be chosen as a basis for evaluating the process of development of the structure of the organisation. Unfortunately, much of the current literature is - at best - superficial in its analysis and - at worst - a considerable portion would be more honestly filed under the heading of fringe religion rather than management science. This may well be attributed to the fact that many managerial writers are now career academics who have little or no experience within the commercial enterprise.

Greiner (1972) identified five "key dimensions" in the evolution of the enterprise:

- **Age of the organization.**
- **Size of the organization.**
- **Stages of evolution.**
- **Stages of revolution.**
- **Growth rate of the industry.**

Greiner postulates that companies pass through alternating phases of **evolution** and *revolution* as their organisations develop:

- **Growth through creativity**
- *Crisis of leadership*

- **Growth through direction**
- *Crisis of autonomy*

- **Growth through delegation**
- *Crisis of control*

- **Growth through coordination**
- *Crisis of red tape*

- **Growth through collaboration**
- *Crisis of ?*

He suggests that this sequence of development is common through all industry but that the pace of each stage is dependent on the market environment of the enterprise. In rapidly developing technologies, periods of evolution will be relatively brief whilst in mature industries with secure profitability evolutionary development will be much more sustained. In general this view matches the consensus of the management literature.

What is less accepted latterly, particularly in the recent literature, is Greiner's contention that the sequence of development described above is irreversible. Such titles as **Reengineering the corporation** (Hammer and Champy 1993), **When giants learn to dance** (Kanter 1989), **Liberation management** (Peters 1992) have as their central theme that it is possible, and indeed necessary, to restore the values of the entrepreneurial company in the mature organisation.

The general consensus in the management literature is that reconstruction of the organisation of manufacturing systems is both possible and often desirable. Where it is possible, it gives powerful competitive advantages. John Naisbitt (1993) subtitles his book *Global Paradox: The bigger the world economy the more powerful its smallest players.*

The reorganisation of manufacturing systems into smaller operating units is possible, but its implementation is threatened by a number of powerful structural factors. These are often compounded by attitudinal problems which derive from the culture of the organisation. It may well be that there is a dearth of engineering expertise at the strategic decision-making level of the organisation (Brandon 1992a). This leads to two possible adverse consequences: the benefits of technological change may be over-estimated, leading to disillusionment and recrimination when these illusory benefits are not realised; failure to estimate the complexity of the task may lead to its trivialisation and insufficient provision of resources and managerial commitment.

Assuming that this problem is recognised, the problem for the corporate centre may be posed in the form (Brandon 1992b):

Key problems for corporate strategists are:

> *Rationalising the structure of the enterprise to provide suitable conditions for introduction of new technology;*
>
> *Identification, and empowerment, of suitable personnel to drive the programmes of change;*
>
> *Changing the corporate culture so that the conflicts between personal and corporate values are reconciled (Atkinson 1990).*

In the present context, it is axiomatic that evolution is intolerant of states which may be viable when judged in isolation but which have no logical predecessor: to every descendant corresponds a chain of ancestors. Thus new management structures which are intended to reverse the natural evolutionary process must be introduced into the organisation in contravention of the prevailing culture.

REFERENCES

P E Atkinson, 1990, Creating Culture Change: The Key to Successful Total Quality Management, IFS, Bedford England.
J A Brandon, 1992a, Structural impediments to strategic change in the technological enterprise, Journal of Strategic Change, 1(6), 333-9.

J A Brandon, 1992b, Strategic Perspectives for Implementation of FMS, Robotics and CIM, 29th International Machine Tool Design and Research Conference, Macmillan, London, 241-247.

J A Brandon, 1992c, Managing Change in Manufacturing Systems, Productivity Publishing, Olney, England.

L E Greiner, 1972 (July-August), Evolution and revolution as organizations grow, Harvard Business Review, 37-46.

M Hammer and J Champy, 1993, Reengineering the corporation: A manifesto for business revolution, Nicholas Brearley, London.

R M Kanter, 1989, When giants learn to dance: Mastering the challenge of Strategy, Management and Careers in the 1990s, Simon and Schuster, London.

J Naisbitt, 1993, Global Paradox: The bigger the world economy the more powerful its smallest players, Nicholas Brearley, London

T Peters, 1992, Liberation management: Necessary Disorganisation for the Nanosecond Nineties, Pan Macmillan, London.

REASSESSING TAYLOR

As has been decribed, Taylor's first public demonstration of High-Speed Steel illustrated the way in which the new technologies could no longer tolerate the organisational traditions of the nineteenth century. He recognised that the kind of radical restructuring which was necessary to take advantage of new technologies could only be achieved by a new form of corporate structure.

It would be facile even to suggest that he was the first to reach these conclusions. Indeed, similar ideas had long been current in European management circles. Adam Smith (1723-90), the economist, believed that once the management of the enterprise ceased to be the concern of the owner and passed into the control of directors of a joint stock company:

> *Negligence and profusion .... must always prevail more or less, in the management of the affairs of such a company .... The only trades which it seems possible for a joint stock company to carry on successfully, without an exclusive privilege, are those, of which all the operations are capable of being reduced to such a uniformity of method as admits of little or no variation.*

In quoting this passage Clutterbuck and Crainer (1990) suggest that: *In one passage, therefore, Smith criticised what is now the conventional form of industrial ownership and laid the foundations of what was to be called "scientific management".*

The actual extent of Taylor's contribution is extremely difficult to evaluate because of his apparent tendency to assimilate the ideas of others (in particular Charles Babbage) and to rewrite his ideas and reinterpret his anecdotes whenever their truth was challenged. Taylor's biographer (Nelson 1980):

> *Taylor altered or expanded his accounts whenever it suited his immediate purpose. Though all of the stories in the Principles of Scientific Management had a factual basis, they were, with the possible exception of the Simonds episode, approximations of the actual events.*

Nelson describes the Principles of Scientific Management as follows:

> *It was inaccurate in historical detail and, more seriously, in its assertions about the nature of Taylor's contribution and the character of Scientific Management. Taylor's `principles' had little or no relevance to his work, and his suggestion that time study constituted a `science' were hyperbole at best.*

In many respects the ideas of his contemporaries, including Frank and Lilian Gilbreth, have much more claim to scientific validity. For example, the Gilbreths pioneered the use of ideograms to record the sequence of activity of employees and recognised the equivalence of continuous monitoring and activity sampling.

Furthermore, it should be realised that, whereas Taylor himself presented Scientific Management as a coherent overall management philosophy which entailed radical restructuring of the enterprise, his clients - and indeed his associates and partners - often selected only those features of Scientific Management which suited their purpose. All too often the more controversial and industrially adversarial aspects were chosen. Thus it became common for the generally divisive piece-rate system to be introduced without any of the compensatory practices which tended to improve the job of the production operative (Nelson 1980). In this respect at least it is not reasonable to equate Taylor with Taylorism. For example, Clutterbuck and Crainer (1990) quote the *basic principles of effective supervision* of Douglas McCallum, a railroad engineer in the USA in the 1850s:

1. A proper division of responsibilities

2. Sufficient power conferred to enable the same to be fully carried out, that such responsibilities may be real in their character

3. The means of knowing whether such responsibilities are faithfully executed

4. Great promptness in the report of all dereliction of duty, that evils may at once be corrected

5. Such information to be obtained through a series of daily reports and checks that will not embarrass principal officers, nor lessen their influence with their subordinates

6. The adoption of a system, as a whole, which will not only enable the General Superintendent to detect errors immediately, but will also point out the delinquent. "

Why, then, should the key ideas of Scientific Management be important for the understanding of cellular manufacturing systems? Whether or not we may attribute the radical change in the organisation of manufacture in the early years of the twentieth century to Taylor, Taylorism is a symbol for the type of authoritarian hierarchical management structures which have proved extremely robust in the struggle to introduce more advanced organisational concepts.

Taylor's activities as a consultant brought him into conflict with the American Society of Mechanical Engineers where a number of members of council developed the view that he was exploiting the society for commercial gain. Their publications board declined to publish several of his later works (Nelson 1980). (Later in his life the patents on High-Speed Steel were extinguished because he had insisted on a fee to appear as a witness in an infringement case). One of his principal opponents was L. P. Alford, the secretary of the society. As a consequence, wherever Alford supports Taylor's views it may be taken positively.

Alford defined four *Laws of Manufacturing Management* (Alford 1940, p53 - see also Jaffe 1984):

1 Law of specialisation: (specialisation of the job) reducing the number of the mental or manual operations for each job improves quality and increases output.

2 Law of division of effort: (specialisation of the individual) assignment of very few mental or manual tasks that the worker is particularly adapted to perform improves quality and increases output.

This implies that as responsibility is narrowed efficiency is improved.

3 Law of transfer of skill: (specialisation of tools and machines) The skill and attention a tool or machine require are inverse to the skill transferred to the mechanism.

4 Law of Simplification: Restricting the range to a single product or a few types or sizes tends to improve quality and lower production costs.

It may well be that Taylor was the first to articulate these ideas in a coherent form, but the law of transfer of skill is implicit in the development of simplified semi-automatic machine tools by Eli Whitney to manufacture firearms.

It is often suggested that Taylorism has been discredited and superseded. However the influential American writer Robert Waterman suggests that many people talk post-Taylorism whilst their organisations act very traditionally. It should be recognised that Alford's **first law** is extremely similar to Skinner's (1974) third *basic concept (qv.) (Simplicity and repetition breed competence)* and that Alford's fourth law is similar to Skinner's third: *change required in manufacturing (Learning to focus each plant on a limited, concise, manageable set of products, technologies, volumes, and markets).*

Whatever Taylor's own contribution, it is certainly true that a central theme of manufacturing management in the twentieth century has been that of Taylorism. This has been summarised by Rosenbrock (1990), who comments:

> *.. Taylorism has three main components:*
>
> *i. Improvements in working, and in machines, which offer the benefit of greater production for an unchanged human effort. Taylorism takes credit for these improvements, even when they are independent of its other aspects and could be obtained without them.*

ii. A number of techniques to allow the employer to redefine the contract of employment to his own advantage. This can increase the intensity of work and alter the distribution of benefits to the disadvantage of the worker. The just distribution of the rewards provided by modern technology is a political problem, and no existing system meets with full acceptance by all participants.

iii. The withdrawal of control and initiative from the lower levels of an organisation, and their concentration, to the greatest possible extent, in the higher levels. This entails the simplification of tasks, and their precise definition, which assist in their subsequent mechanisation.

(Rosenbrock 1990)

Not surprisingly, perhaps, Lenin was reported to be a considerable admirer of the Taylor system (Clutterbuck and Crainer 1990).

Drucker (1988, pp275-8) identifies two principal weaknesses of Scientific Management:

The belief that analysis of work into simple constituent motions must inevitably be followed by synthesis in terms of individual motions is a fallacy;

The divorce of planning from doing ".. reflects a dubious philosophical concept of an elite which has a monopoly on esoteric knowledge entitling it to manipulate an unwashed peasantry."

REFERENCES

L P Alford, 1940, Principles of Industrial Management, The Ronald Press, New York.

D Clutterbuck and S Crainer, 1990, Makers of Management, Macmillan, London (24-30).

P F Drucker, 1988, The Practice of Management, Heinemann, (originally published 1954).

P F Drucker, 1974, Management: Tasks, Responsibilities, Practices, Heinemann.

W J Jaffe, 1984 (April), Standardization and Scientific Management, Mechanical Engineering, pp56-59.

D Nelson, 1980, Frederick W. Taylor and the rise of Scientific Management, University of Wisconsin Press.

H Rosenbrock, 1990, Machines with a Purpose, Oxford University Press.

W Skinner, 1974 (May-June), The focused factory, Harvard Business Review, 113-121; also in V Bignell et al. (Editors), 1985, Manufacturing Systems: Context, Applications and Techniques, Open University /Blackwell, Oxford.

THE PHOENIX ARISES

As has been described, one of the key principles of Taylorism is the concentration on the individual as the primary managerial focus. One powerful justification for this viewpoint is that the existing group-focused organisational structures impeded progress. Only by destroying the power of the group could management gain control of the organisation to enable introduction of new technology.

What was underestimated was the robustness of the group under threat.

Antony Jay, best known (with Jonathan Lynn) for his political satires *Yes Minister* and *Yes Prime Minister*, spent a number of years as a management consultant after working in production roles in the British Broadcasting Corporation. He has presented the experience gained in a number of books including **Management and Machiavelli** and **Effective Presentation**. His most relevant work in the current context is **Corporation Man** (Jay 1972). In this work he calls upon biological and anthropological evidence, citing Konrad Lorenz, Desmond Morris and (particularly) Robert Ardrey, for the view that natural human organisational patterns are still dominated by the values of the hunting party. Within the group, cooperation is essential to achieve common objectives; competition between groups, often implicitly aggressively, may be inevitable, particularly when resources are scarce. Inheriting from the hunting party, Jay suggests that the ten-group is a typical operational size for a cooperative activity.

Although he reached this insight independently, Jay was certainly not the first to identify the power of autonomous groups in the managerial context. Perhaps the best documented studies are those undertaken by Elton Mayo and his co-workers in the

Hawthorne plant of the Western Electric Company in the late 1920s and early 1930s (Roethlisberger and Dickson 1939).

Whilst the Hawthorne studies are now perceived as being concerned with evaluating psychological and sociological theories, it is apparent, from reading the original texts rather than modern commentaries, that the original motivations were rather narrower and more aligned towards Scientific Management. For example, the study which induced the researchers to question their basic assumptions was an assessment of illumination on productivity. It was the unforeseen outcome, rather than initial hypotheses, of these experiments that led the Harvard researchers to formulate their theories concerning the necessity to view work as a cooperative activity. For example Mayo (1949) commented:

A highly competent group of Western Electric engineers refused to accept defeat when experiments to demonstrate the effect of illumination on work seemed to lead nowhere. The conditions of scientific experiment had apparently been fulfilled - experimental room, control room; changes introduced one at a time; all other conditions held steady. And the results were perplexing: Roethisberger gives two instances - lighting improved in the experimental room, production went up; but it rose also in the control room. The opposite of this: lighting diminished from 10 to 3 foot-candles in the experimental room and production again went up; simultaneously in the control room, with illumination constant, production also rose.

The second phase of the Hawthorne studies was an interview programme where the researchers interviewed employees about their attitudes to work, the company and their colleagues. Mayo makes it clear that this was a consequence of the disappointing outcome of the scientific experiments.

As with a number of contributions to the management literature, there have been serious doubts raised about the objectivity of reporting of a number of the significant researchers in the Hawthorne studies. For example, many of the discoveries attributed to Elton Mayo were actually those of members of staff at Western Electric rather than external researchers and took place before he even visited the site of the Hawthorne experiments.

Much of the analysis provided by Mayo and his co-workers was preconditioned by Mayo's rather unconventional views on the physiological and psychological attributes of the workers and are not supported by the contemporary reports and interview records in the Hawthorne archive (Gillespie 1991). Roethlisberger (op. cit. p.147) attributes the reluctance of supervisors to change their attitudes as due to *....classic infantile conflict of outward submission to one's parents combined with inner rebellion. He ...was not in a position to judge the objective complaints of the supervisors in the course of the interviews;...* Apparently these were something of an irrelevant nuisance. Not surprisingly, the enthusiasm for the research of Mayo and his colleagues was not universal throughout the Hawthorne plants.

The central finding of the researchers in the Hawthorne studies, if it is acceptable to distil the work of *between seventy-five and a hundred investigators* (Clutterbuck and Crainer 1990) into a single sentence, was that the behaviour of groups cannot be inferred by aggregating the behaviour of individuals studied in isolation. This undermines one of the central tenets of Scientific Management that work can be analysed in terms of observation of skilled operatives, breaking their activities into elementary operations which may then be synthesised into efficient standards. Taylor specified explicitly that it was preferable that the individuals study should be *... in as many separate establishments and different parts of the country ...* thereby excluding intentionally any possibility that the workers had developed any group values.

The sociologists D. C. Miller and W. H. Form summarised the work of Mayo in terms of eight principles:

1. Work is a group activity;

2. Work forms the pattern of adult social activity;

3. Group identity is more important than working conditions;

4. A complaint may reflect insecurity of status rather than an objective response to events;

5. Attitudes and effectiveness are affected by social pressures;

6. Informal groups exercise strong social controls;

7. Change from a structured to an adaptive society affects the social organisation within the factory;

8. Group collaboration must be developed otherwise it will evolve independently.

(Derived from Brown 1954).

Brown (1954) constructed three influential viewpoints on Mayos' conclusions:

- *The Industrialist: they are true but irrelevant;*

    The justification for this viewpoint is that knowledge about the social systems of an organisation does little to improve its profitability, which - after all - is the primary focus of management. Brown points to businesses in the same industry with grossly different productivity. He contends that understanding the social systems may well be the key to unlocking this unexplained latent productivity benefit.

- *The Social Psychologist: they are true but obvious;*

    Brown suggests that: *in accepting the work of Mayo his only criticism is that all this was known long ago.* Where Mayo contributes to knowledge is in placing it in the context of the industrial firm.

- *The Sociologist: they are true but they do not go far enough.*

    In many respects, this criticism anticipates the whole of the analysis of Gillespie (1991), nearly forty years later. As Brown remarked, Roethlisberger and Dickson were criticised, for ignoring trade union issues, in the review of their book published in the American Journal of Sociology in July 1940.

The preoccupation with the individual, resulting from the ideas of Taylor and his contemporaries, led to the evolution of informal social structures which, in the absence of control from the top, set their own values and attitudes. Jay (1972) described this in the following terms:

> *The result, therefore, of the instrumental approach to managing large concentrations of men is to force the growth of a natural organisation of ten-groups in opposition. The corporation then has two management structures - the official one it draws up and circulates, and the one on the factory floor that controls the work....*

So how much have industrial managers learned from history? Not very much, if the views of Krackhardt and Hanson (1993) are to be accepted. They contend:

- *That the actual interactions within a company can only be understood with reference to a multiplicity of overlaid networks;*

- *That the informal networks are often significantly more influential in determining individual behaviour than the formal hierarchy;*

- *That senior management are usually ignorant of the true interactions between the formal and the informal controls of the organisation.*

They suggest a number of techniques for analysis of networks with typical structures. As with many of the authors whose ideas contribute to the current volume, they use a biological metaphor, that the formal structure of the organisation is its skeleton but that its informal networks are its central nervous system.

References

J A C Brown, 1954, The Social Psychology of Industry, Penguin, Harmondsworth.

R Gillespie, 1991, Manufacturing knowledge: A history of the Hawthorne experiments, Cambridge, England.

A Jay, 1972, Corporation Man, Jonathan Cape, London.

D Krackhardt and J R Hanson, July- August 1993, Informal networks: the company behind the chart, Harvard Business Review, 104-111.

E Mayo, 1949, Social problems of an industrial civilization, Routledge, London (see also the extract in D S Pugh (Editor), 1971, Organization Theory, Penguin, Harmondsworth, 215-229).

F J Roethlisberger and W J Dickson, 1939, Management and the Worker, Harvard University Press.

THE ANACHRONISTIC FACTORY

In the early 1970s two significant research papers appeared with the same title - which is chosen here again - The Anachronistic Factory. The first, in the Harvard Business Review, by Wickham Skinner (1971) of the Harvard Business School, approached the key problem addressed in the current text, that of the mismatch of technological capability and management infrastructure, from the viewpoint of the manager. In a deliberately titled response, the British engineer Theo Williamson (1972) approached the problem from the perspective of the engineer. Latterly, the author (Brandon 1994) has sought to evaluate the lasting significance of these two major contributions and project another vision for the next twenty years.

What Skinner describes as the "Piecemeal syndrome" would be familiar to manufacturing systems engineers, before and since, by using a case study of an anonymous manufacturing company. Quite understandably, their focus of attention was the problem which was currently perceived as inhibiting their effectiveness. However, the solution of a series of problems led to a sequence of plant modernisations involving substantial automation of production facilities but which failed to improve productivity. This turned the focus away from technology onto the management information system. Once a new planning and scheduling system was installed, deficiencies in human relations became apparent.

Whilst all this was going on, however, the company's market had not been waiting on the outcome. Product cycles had shortened together with an increasing demand for variety. Not surprisingly, this necessitated revision of the production technology, manufacturing organisation and personnel management within the company:

The entire period of time represented six and a half years of frustration, inadequacy, and the constant pressure of making changes. In the end, the system needed as much revision as it had in the beginning. During no single year were results even marginally satisfactory. Stockholders, managers, employees and engineers shared only one mutual sentiment - that of unrelenting dissatisfaction.

As has been suggested, the overwhelming majority of employees in manufacturing industry will recognise the process described by Skinner from experience in their own companies. Again, either from experience or awareness of practice elsewhere, many personnel will be aware that there is another way, currently referred to as Concurrent Engineering (q.v.).

The ideas of Concurrent Engineering have been on the managerial agenda for many years. For example, Peter Drucker clearly described in the early 1950s a system of organisation that would immediately be classified as Concurrent Engineering.

It is disconcerting to read not only a clear description of Concurrent Engineering forty years ago but also that much of the current terminology - such as "task forces" - was already in use. It is, perhaps, paradoxical that in a much more recent work Drucker (1992) seems to regard Concurrent Engineering as an organisational pattern for the future.

What is obviously lacking, in the example presented by Skinner, is evidence that the management of engineering is integrated into the corporate strategy. Brandon (1992a) has suggested that the lack of engineers amongst corporate management is a significant disadvantage in enabling this process. Even where companies do have an engineering representation at board level, their skills are often so out of date that reliance on their expertise would, in itself, be a threat to corporate well-being.

Skinner cites a common factor - *a kind of Murphy's Law* - to a wide range of ineffective automation projects:

An inconsistency or lack of congruence in any one of dozens of ingredients in the system will often ruin the performance and utility of the whole. These are not just technical or engineering problems, but also problems of marketing, scheduling, engineering, inventory, changeover, cost control, accounting, volume sensitivity, worker acceptance, training, supervision, safety, wage system, motivation, union contract, utilities, maintenance, pollution/effluents, community relations, vendor requirements, plant organization structure, executive performance evaluation, and communications and information flows.

In short, everything counts. One subtle flaw may immobilize or neutralize the benefits of an otherwise marvellously planned and conceived project.

Skinner concludes that the incremental change processes most common in the development of manufacturing systems are inevitably destined for failure. Only by taking a total system approach can programmes of organisational change have any chance of being successful.

Skinner classified the changes needed in manufacturing into two groups:

1. Changes in conventional concepts of managing manufacturing.

2. Changes in meeting human needs in manufacturing careers.

CHALLENGING ACCEPTED TRUTHS

To illustrate the changes needed in conventional concepts, Skinner identifies seven *myths and assumptions* which must be challenged in order to progress change strategies:

1 That the primary performance criteria should be cost and efficiency:

Whilst Skinner, quite properly, links cost and efficiency together, there is some merit in discussing them separately here.

The problem of development of costing systems has proved to be one of the least tractable of problems in manufacturing systems engineering. Recently, a number of authors have advocated the general abandonment of the costing systems used in manufacturing. Of these, perhaps the most influential has been the text by Johnson and Kaplan (1987). They contend that the effectiveness of the manufacturing enterprise is inhibited by inappropriate costing systems which originate from the managerial needs of the nineteenth century but which have been perpetuated, largely unchanged, to the present day:

> *By 1925, American industrial firms had developed virtually every management accounting procedure known today. The procedures were developed in just over one hundred years by managers seeking information about opportunities for gain in hierarchies......*

> *After 1925 a subtle change occurred in the information used by managers to direct the affairs of complex hierarchies. Until the 1920s, managers invariably relied on information about the underlying processes, transactions and events that produce financial numbers. By the 1960s and 1970s, however, managers commonly relied on the financial numbers alone.*

As a result of the extensive criticism of traditional management accounting methods, particularly by Robert Kaplan and his associates (Kaplan 1984, 1986, 1988, Cooper and Kaplan 1988, Cooper 1989), a new methodology of production costing has been developed, that of Activity-Based Costing (Innes et al. 1994). The fundamental principle of activity-based costing is that cost apportionment should match, as far as possible, the consumption of resources. In particular, the crude apportionment into categories of direct and indirect costs should be significantly refined.

Whether or not the term itself is new, activity-based costing is far from a new idea. For example, Drucker (1955) emphasised the merits of Transaction-Based Costing systems in the 1950s.

There was considerable justification for the traditional approach to manufacturing costing, based on the loading of labour costs with a representative overhead cost, at a time when labour costs typically formed 40% of overall costs. However, with such products as computers the labour cost may be as little as 1% of aggregate cost (Yates 1986). Using the labour cost as a basis for accounting can no longer be tolerated.

Without sophisticated computational aids, the costs of calculating accurate costings were unacceptable when compared to the accruing benefits. When every manager has a powerful computer, with sophisticated spreadsheets, on his/her desk, the potential for accurate dynamic costing can no longer be disregarded.

Turning now to the subject of efficiency, which Skinner quite rightly links to costs, it is gradually being recognised that it is much more important to measure effectiveness. Unfortunately efficiency is easy to measure whereas effectiveness is not. The fact that a thing is easy to measure does not, in itself, mean that it is a desirable focus for management (Small 1983a).

Returning to labour costs, the most common focus of efficiency measures, these have usually been a constant subject of incremental improvement over many years; further benefits are only likely to accrue from an inordinate expenditure of effort or a complete change of process - entailing revolution rather than evolution (Foster 1986, Brandon 1992b). Effectiveness is about identifying those variables to be measured which give real competitive advantage rather than marginal improvements in internal measures of performance.

2 That it is possible to satisfy a wide range of performance measures:

Skinner cites: low costs, high quality, minimum investment, short cycle times, high flexibility, and rapid introduction of new products.

This is a subject to which Skinner returned in his frequently cited paper "The Focused Factory" (1974) and forms the subject of the next chapter.

3 That the management of manufacturing facilities is essentially a job for engineers:

Whilst it is obviously essential that technologists should contribute to the design of manufacturing systems, long-held assumptions about their role should be questioned. Skinner suggests that they may well be: ... *inadequately trained and oriented toward human and social factors, financial problems, and the strategy and markets of the entire firm.*

4 Mechanization is a specialized task for industrial engineers and operations researchers:

It may well be that the scientific basis for these specialised disciplines leads to their practitioners' projecting a specious image of the power and effectiveness of their techniques. In practice, however, limitations of the methods may lead to serious, perhaps fatal, compromises to the competitiveness of the manufacturing system. Because of the authority of the specialists, real or assumed, it is often difficult for a non-specialist to challenge or refute results from simulations of various options for change to the organisation of the manufacturing systems.

5 That abstract methodologies - Skinner refers to the *systems approach and a high level of conceptualization* - can substitute for experience and process based knowledge:

As has been noted above (Johnson and Kaplan 1987), one of the key disciplines of manufacturing systems engineering, that of management accounting, has become abstracted to the point where the measures have little or no relevance to the underlying technological processes.

6 That the replacement of people with machines is either necessary or desirable for its own sake:

Skinner suggested that there was a whole body of recent experience which refuted this contention.

7 That economic analysis will always favour machines:

There is a wide body of anecdotal evidence that this is no longer an acceptable assumption. Consider, for example, the experience at Schlumberger Manufacturing:

> *The results did not require sophisticated computer applications. In fact we turned off our shop floor computer, adopted a manual floor-control approach, and cancelled a $400,000 automation project.*
>
> (Ashton and Cook 1989)

Since Skinner's paper, there has been a growing body of opinion that, far from assisting investment in Advanced Manufacturing Technology, traditional investment appraisal methodologies are biased against innovation. In particular, it is difficult to quantify so-called *intangible benefits* which accrue in integrated systems but which are absent in traditional organisations. These include: customer responsiveness, reductions in quality conformance costs, elimination of supervision activities, etc. Often these are assigned as indirect costs in traditional systems, and their management is accorded only superficial attention. Kaplan (1986) suggests that the problem may not be the techniques of discounted cash flow themselves but rather how they are applied.

Suresh and Meredith (1985) argue that the inclusion of intangible costs in investment appraisal is essential but that it can only be achieved if it becomes a strategic rather than an operational activity. Canada (1986) and Hamblin and Hundy (1986) develop methods for analysing and presenting investment appraisals in advance manufacturing technology which remove the bias against innovation. Small (1983b) provides practical guidance in balancing the differing impact on the organisation of the essentially local effects maintaining incremental investment in traditional technology and the much more radical impact of the introduction of advanced manufacturing systems.

MEETING HUMAN NEEDS

Skinner provided a simple checklist of key problems in the anachronistic factory:

> *Pay systems based on hours worked.*
>
> *Physical arrangements to treat employees with disrespect and supervisory assumptions which fail to treat them as individuals.*
>
> *Decision-making processes that leave out the opinions and ideas of involved employees.*
>
> *Promotion and job-security policies that emphasise only experience and seniority.*
>
> *Communications practices that withhold information or present only one point of view.*
>
> *Job designs and work content that focus solely on motor-mechanism/ physiological aspects of an employee's capacities and leave out the emotional and spiritual dimensions.*
>
> *Union contracts and governance systems that restrict change and stifle initiative.*

This can be summarised:

NOT ONLY IS SCIENTIFIC MANAGEMENT NOT THE SOLUTION TO THE ORGANISATIONAL PROBLEMS OF THE ANACHRONISTIC FACTORY - IT IS A SIGNIFICANT PART OF THE PROBLEM

FROM DIAGNOSIS TO PROGNOSIS

Skinner, the management specialist, provided a thorough diagnosis of the defects of the anachronistic factory. Williamson, an engineering practitioner, provided a vision for the future.

Like Frederick Taylor, Williamson contributed to both production technology and production management. As leader of the engineering design team at Molins, Williamson is credited with the development of the world's first flexible manufacturing system (FMS), the System 24. Small (1983a) suggests that at least half of Williamson's paper describing the design issues of System 24 (Williamson 1968) could well have been presented fifteen years later:

> *If he had written it today he would have titled it FMS and half of the paper could have remained the same. Most of the concepts are still valid, although we have more technology, particularly in handling systems, to apply to the task.*

It is interesting to note that Williamson had commented that the inadequacy of production technology was a hindrance to progress in the 1950s:

> *The design of machine tools has not changed radically for many years and is, in general, unsuitable for very accurate numerical control.*
>
> (quoted in the authoritative study by Carter and Williams (1957)).

Brandon and Al-Shareef (1992) have presented an analysis of the technological development of manufacturing systems consistent with Skinner's analysis of the anachronistic factory. In the review cited, for example, it is suggested that the optimisation of spindle bearing systems reached a natural pause due to the achievement of many objectives and the realisation that others could not be reached without unacceptable effort. They quoted Carter and William's (1957) on the invention of the transfer machine by Taylor and Woolard in 1923-5:

> *Though they produced excellent work they were not to be relied on day in day out because their ancillary equipment - electric, hydraulic and pneumatic - had not been sufficiently developed.*

The designers of System 24 met similar limitations, finding that existing machine tools could not achieve the necessary cutting speeds to obtain maximum benefit from the light alloys they were machining and the capability of new cutting-tool materials. Their solution was to develop new machine tools which were capable of achieving the surface cutting speeds required. Whereas with Taylor the new technology demanded new methods of production organisation, for Williamson organisational pressures stimulated the invention of new production technology. In turn, the demands of the new machines triggered creative activity directed towards the structure of the manufacturing systems.

As with System 24, over and over again the literature supports Skinner's contention that successful change in manufacturing systems engineering demands simultaneous analysis of production technology and manufacturing infrastructure.

WILLIAMSON'S VISION

For reasons which will become clear, the technical detail of System 24 will be deferred to a later section. As has been suggested above, Williamson anticipated many of the developments in the design of manufacturing systems and their organisational environment which have taken place subsequently.

A key insight, which could be easily overlooked, is the way in which multinational organisations - Williamson cites as a particular culprit the motor industry - impose standardised organisation patterns on their manufacturing systems. Whilst certain industrial processes demand that operators effectively serve the machine - for example in transfer machines for metal cutting of such components as engine blocks - the same organisational controls have been extended to contexts where such subordination is not a technological necessity. Williamson cites as a particular example of a degrading and dehumanising activity the feeding and unloading of press tools:

> *It is difficult to imagine a more inappropriate activity for man as a thinking animal to require, on the one hand, that he expend a major portion of his life-energy in total slavery to a clanging, banging, unforgiving metal monster, knowing that, on the other hand, man at his best can only poorly serve the machine, and that he really intrudes negatively upon the machine's efficiency. The machine is prevented from operating round-the-clock and at higher speeds by its dependence on man, and its very nature, operating philosophy and configuration could be optimized to the task in hand if it were not still regarded as an extension of man's hands.*

Once again, the complete solution to this problem must involve both the machine and its operator within the organisational context of the whole manufacturing system.

It is interesting to note that Womack et al. (1990), in their immensely influential text, reject Volvo's variation in the form of their model of lean production:

> *We have not audited Udevalla or Kalmar, the two plants operated on the neocraft model, but some simple arithmetic suggests that if ten workers require 8 hours simply to assemble four vehicles (not including welding the body, painting it, and gathering necessary materials) - for a total of 20 assembly hours per vehicle - Udevalla can hardly hope to compete with our survey's leading lean-production plant, which requires only 13.3 hours to weld, paint, and assemble a slightly smaller and less elaborate vehicle.*

It is, to say the least, surprising that such a respected and influential group of researchers should simply dismiss an experiment which was intended to provide an alternative model to their own *lean production* scenario for the future of the motor industry.

Williamson suggested that Scientific Management created Taylorism as a self-fulfilling prophecy. If the employee is to be treated as a component in a production machine then the only applicants for such jobs are those who will be content to act in that capacity.

Reviewed from over twenty years later, Williamson's paper abounds in missed opportunities. For example, in discussion of press tools he mentions that they ... *can be designed to have their dies changed very quickly*... Taiichi Ohno, of Toyota, came to the same conclusion in making Single Minute Exchange of Dies (SMED) one of the essential features of the Toyota Production System (Shingo 1981).

Another feature of the Toyota Production System which was clearly in Williamson's mind was the concept of Just In Time production.

Williamson recognised that investment in advanced manufacturing technology, and in particular flexible manufacturing systems, would be inhibited unless a new approach were taken to investment appraisal. He suggested that, whereas a dedicated transfer

48

machine becomes obsolete as soon as the component which it is designed to produce is discontinued, typically five to seven years in motor manufacture, flexible machines can be reallocated to other products and should be depreciated over much longer timescales.

References

J E Ashton and F X Cook Jr., 1989 (March-April), Time to reform job shop manufacturing, Harvard Business Review, 106-111.

J A Brandon, 1992a, Structural impediments to strategic change in the technological enterprise, Journal of Strategic Change, 1(6), 1992, 333-9.

J A Brandon, 1992b, Managing change in manufacturing systems, Productivity Publishing, Olney, England.

J A Brandon, 1994, The anachronistic factory revisited, International Journal of Advanced Manufacturing Technology,

J A Brandon and K J H Al-Shareef, 1992, Optimization of machine tool spindle-bearing systems: a critical review, Transactions of the American Society of Mechanical Engineers, Journal of Engineering for Industry, 114(5) 244-253.

J R Canada, 1986 (March), Non-Traditional Method for Evaluating CIM Opportunities Assigns Weight to Intangibles, Industrial Engineering, 66-71.

C F Carter and B R Williams, 1957, Industry and Technical Progress: Factors Governing the Speed of Application of Science, Oxford University Press.

R Cooper and R S Kaplan, 1988 (September-October), Measure costs right: make the right decisions, Harvard Business Review, 96-103.

R Cooper, 1989 (January-February), You need a new cost system when..., Harvard Business Review, 77-82.

P F Drucker, 1954, The practice of management, Heinemann, London.

P F Drucker, 1992, Managing for the future, Butterworth- Heinemann, Oxford.

R Foster, 1986, Innovation: the attacker's advantage, Macmillan, London.

J Innes, F Mitchell and T Yoshikawa, 1994, Activity Based Costing for Engineers, Research Studies Press, Taunton/ John Wiley, Chichester.

H T Johnson and R S Kaplan, 1987, Relevance lost: the rise and fall of management accounting, Harvard Business School Press.

R S Kaplan, 1984 (July-August), Yesterday's accounting undermines production, Harvard Business Review, 95-101.

R S Kaplan, 1986 (March-April), Must CIM be justified by faith alone? Harvard Business Review, 87-94.

R S Kaplan, 1988 (January-February), One cost system isn't enough, Harvard Business Review, 61-66.

M Porter, 1987 (May-June), From competitive advantage to corporate strategy, Harvard Business Review, 43-59.

S Shingo, 1981, Study of Toyota Production System from Industrial Engineering Viewpoint, Japan Management Association, Tokvo.

W Skinner, 1971, (January-February), The anachronistic factory, Harvard Business Review, 61-70.

W Skinner, 1974 (May-June), The focused factory, Harvard Business Review, 113-121; also in V Bignell et al. (Editors), 1985, Manufacturing Systems: Context, Applications and Techniques, Open University /Blackwell, Oxford.

B W Small, 1983a, Wealth generation - our essential task, Proceedings of the Institution of Mechanical Engineers, 197(B) 131-141.

B W Small, 1983b, Paying for the Technology - Making the Intangibles, Tangible, Proceedings of the Second European Conference on Advanced Manufacturing (Editor B W Rooks), 183-187

N C Suresh and J R Meredith, 1985, Justifying Multimachine Systems: An Integrated Strategic Approach, Journal of Manufacturing Systems, 4(2), 117-134.

D T N Williamson, 1968, The pattern of batch manufacture and its influence on machine tool design, Proceedings of the Institution of Mechanical Engineers, 182(1) 870-895.

D T N Williamson, 1972, The anachronistic factory, Proceedings of the Royal Society, A331, 139-160.

A Yates, 1986, Evaluation of advanced manufacturing technology, in: Managing advanced manufacturing technology, Editor C A Voss, IFS/Springer-Verlag, Bedford England, 225-239.

THE FOCUSED FACTORY

Although this section will concentrate largely on the analysis of Skinner (1974), once again the key ideas have been articulated over and over again, both before and since. For example, Drucker (1955) anticipates both Skinner and the "customer focus" advocates of the 1990s such as Richard Schonberger (1990).

Drucker takes as his example the manufacture of electric capacitors. He notes that, although they may look the same, be the same technically and be manufactured on the same production line, each customer may have different expectations reflected in their performance specifications. Such expectations, Drucker notes, may be far removed from the design requirements of the supplier, citing resistance to termites in the Southern States or to high humidity in the North-West. Put simply, internal perceptions are just inadequate to assess the needs of the end user.

Drucker prescribes seven marketing goals:

1 Competitive appraisal of existing products: market share, comparison with direct and indirect competitors;

2 Setting of target market statistics for the existing products in new markets;

3 Rationalisation of product ranges: abandoning existing products - based on market appraisal, technological analysis, or to match corporate strategy;

4 Development of new products for existing markets: number of products, product features, revenue expectations, and market share;

5 Assessment of new products in new markets: revenue and market share;

6 The structure of the distribution function required to achieve the marketing goals and its pricing policy;

7 Measuring performance in meeting customer aspirations as to value, product acceptance, and the perception of the quality of service provided.

Whilst these are presented, quite rightly, by Drucker as marketing goals, awareness of their importance should pervade the whole organisation.

Skinner chooses a similar example from his own experience in the electronics industry. His chosen example was of a small manufacturer of printed circuits. Their key strength was in production of custom-built circuits in small batches typically less than 100 units. Their twenty or so customers used these products in engineering test and development work. In this market, price was not a particularly important market criterion but delivery performance was crucial.

In an attempt to diversify the business, the company's president accepted an order for 20000 circuit boards, at a price far below its economic order quantity for its traditional business. The expectation was an increase in volume, broadening of the customer base and diversification of the product range.

The outcome was far removed from the president's expectation. The traditional customer base was alienated because of deterioration in quality and degradation in delivery performance. This might have been acceptable if the new customer had been receiving the service promised. In fact the company were unable to manufacture to the agreed cost and found that over a third of deliveries were returned because of inferior quality conformance. The company was forced to refinance the business, and, ultimately, the ownership changed hands.

Obviously, if the company had tested their strategy against Drucker's seven marketing goals then this disaster would not have occurred. Unfortunately, the history of corporate strategy is littered with similar cases. Porter (1988) studied the track record of 33 large US companies over three decades, concluding:

> *The track record of corporate strategies has been dismal... The corporate strategies of most companies have dissipated instead of created shareholder value.*

To two of his earlier challenges to accepted truths Skinner now added a third *basic concept:*

> *(1) There are many ways to compete besides by producing at low cost.*
>
> *(2) A factory cannot perform well by every yardstick.*
>
> *(3) Simplicity and repetition breed competence.*

Skinner (1974) prescribes four basic changes in the management of manufacturing:

> *(1) Seeing the problem not as "How can we increase productivity?" but as "How can we compete?"*
>
> *(2) Seeing the problem as encompassing the efficiency of the entire manufacturing organization, not only the efficiency of the direct labour and the work force. (In most plants, direct labour and the work force represent only a small percentage of total costs.)*
>
> *(3) Learning to focus each plant on a limited, concise, manageable set of products, technologies, volumes, and markets.*
>
> *(4) Learning to structure basic manufacturing policies and supporting services so that they focus on one explicit manufacturing task instead of on many, inconsistent, conflicting, implicit tasks.*

SMALL IS BEAUTIFUL

This section chooses as its theme the title of one of the most influential texts for the environmental movement. The title of E F Schumacher's text (1973) is often quoted, however, as here, without its subtitle: *A study of economics as if people mattered.*

Williamson (1968) used an analogy from biological systems to pass judgement on the development of the factory:

> *.. cells of a living organism do not themselves grow in size, to form one big cell, but duplicate themselves as the organism grows. When abnormally large cells do occasionally form, it presages cancerous growth, and usually results in the eventual death of the organism.*

In manufacturing systems, he continues:

> *Instead of growing in size, as would be logical, by adding self-contained manufacturing of optimum size, which would have preserved much of the original favourable character of the small workshop, whilst increasing the output to any desired degree, the modern batch production factory has just grown bigger geometrically, with lines of milling machines and lines of lathes and lines of drills, and mounting stacks of parts between the lines, waiting to go from machinist to machinist, each of whom has never seen it before, and after carrying out one or two operations, will never see it again!*

In some respects this biological analogy is flawed. If extended it can easily be used to reach a conclusion diametrically opposed to Williamson's. In all non-trivial biological organisms, cells aggregate and specialise: for milling machines read lungs; for lathes read the heart; for drills read other organs. This is a process-based functional organisation!

What is certainly true, however, is that it would be unusual for the process/product organisation model to be a factor in the entrepreneurial organisation (Brandon and Huang 1993). After all, if the company only owns one milling machine it is difficult to arrange it in a line. Thus the process/product bifurcation comes with the successful establishment of the small company. It is likely to occur when managerial attention is otherwise focused and may be delegated to staff who fail to appreciate the importance and potential adverse consequences of this seminal decision.

An essential feature of the analysis of both Skinner (1971) and Williamson (1972) is that any programme of change in a manufacturing organisation must take into account all functions of the enterprise. This is often described as the holistic approach. From a purely logistic point of view the planning of radical change can best be accomplished by a small group of people.

It is essential that the members of any planning group contribute the specialised skills of their functional group without bringing into the activity constraints of vested interest (Brandon 1993).

This approach to integration of engineering functions is extremely topical in manufacturing systems engineering. It is known as *Concurrent* or *Simultaneous Engineering*. Readers of this literature may be astonished to learn that the coordination of engineering functions in a *task force* is clearly described by Peter Drucker in the early 1950s (Drucker 1955). The author has asked (Brandon 1995):

- *If, as was suggested by Drucker, Concurrent Engineering was already the prevailing method of organization of product design in the early 1950s, what (if anything) happened to diminish its distribution?*

- *If Drucker's description is accurate, why has it taken so long for the potential of Concurrent Engineering to become recognized?*

- *In either case, why is Concurrent Engineering only now becoming so topical that it is worthy of academic interest in its own right?*

REFERENCES

J A Brandon, 1993, On the vulnerability of programmes of strategic change to functional interests: A case study, Journal of Strategic Change, 2(3), 151-156.

J A Brandon, 1995, Concurrent Engineeering and Manufacturing Infrastructure, Fifth International Conference: Flexible Automation and Intelligent Manufacturing, Stuttgart, Editors, R D Scraft et al., Begell House, New York.

J A Brandon and G Q Huang, 1993, Use of an Agent-based system for concurrent mechanical design, Chapter 18 in A Kusiak (Editor), Concurrent Engineering: Automation, Tools and Techniques, John Wiley, New York, 463-479.

P F Drucker, 1955, The practice of management, Heinemann, London.

M E Porter, 1988 (Spring), From competitive advantage to corporate strategy, McKinsey Quarterly, 35-66.

R J Schonberger, 1990, Building and chain of customers: linking business functions to create the World Class Company, Hutchinson Business Books, London.

E F Schumacher, 1973, Small is beautiful: a study of economics as if people mattered, Blond and Briggs, London.

W Skinner, 1971 (January-February), The anachronistic factory, Harvard Business Review, 61-70.

W Skinner, 1974 (May-June), The focused factory, Harvard Business Review, 113-121; also in V Bignell et al. (Editors), 1985, Manufacturing Systems: Context, Applications and Techniques, Open University /Blackwell, Oxford.

D T N Williamson, 1968, The pattern of batch manufacture and its influence on machine tool design, Proceedings of the Institution of Mechanical Engineers, 182, 870-895.

D T N Williamson, 1972, The Anachronistic Factory, Proceedings of the Royal Society, Volume A331, 139-160.

SIN, STRUCTURE AND SUBSIDIARITY

No organisation is sounder than the men who run it and who delegate others to run

it. They are in a position to tip the balance in a decentralised organisation toward

centralisation and even one-man rule.

(Alfred P Sloan Jr. 1965).

The **Principle of Subsidiarity** is one which has exercised the politicians of Western Europe for many years but which they have failed to communicate to their constituency. It is indivisible from the concept of **Federalism.** In the U.K. at least there is a perception that the innate nature of federalism implies a trend to a centralised structure. Nothing could be further from the truth.

It is perhaps unusual to invoke religious authorities in a book about manufacturing, but a number of influential authors (for example Schumacher, 1973, and Handy 1989) have used the teachings of the Roman Catholic Church as a basis for understanding the structure and behaviour of federal organisations. Many of the innovators in the present work saw a moral dimension in their endeavours, although not always successfully; for example, Taylor set out to improve the lot of the worker and bequeathed us Taylorism. The principle was expressed in two papal encyclicals (Leo XIII 1891, Pius XII 1941), the latter of which stated:

> *... it is an injustice, a grave evil and a disturbance of right order for a large*
> *and higher organisation to arrogate to itself functions which can be*
> *performed efficiently by smaller and lower bodies.* (quoted from Handy 1989).

Schumacher (1973) interpreted the second encyclical:

> *The Principle of Subsidiary Function implies that the burden of proof lies always on those who want to deprive a lower level of its function , and thereby of its freedom and responsibility in that respect; they have to prove that the lower level is incapable of fulfilling this function satisfactorily and that the higher level can actually do much better.*

Unfortunately, it is a principle more often disregarded than observed.

Taking the most well known federal structure, the government of the United States, it is enshrined in the constitution that *...all powers not expressly granted to the central government were reserved for the states. (The Economist, May 6th 1995, 59).* On a number of occasions the United States Supreme Court has called the Federal Government to account when it has tried to apply national priorities to local issues. Major damage was done in the 1930s to Roosevelt's New Deal. It had been thought that the Court had ceased to guard this aspect of the constitution when Congress cited its authority to regulate commerce across state lines until, in April 1995, the Court reinforced the authority of the states once again by accepting that a 1990 gun control law violated the freedom of individual states.

Handy (1989) took great care to emphasise that federalism should be distinguished from decentralisation. With decentralisation, tasks may be devolved whilst leaving the structures of authority and responsibility undisturbed. Federalism, on the other hand, involves a passing of authority and responsibility to the operating level, resulting in local autonomy. As described by Porter (1987) true devolution of control is rare in corporate strategy. Handy suggests that the federal organisation: *... is culturally different, it requires a different set of attitudes...* He continues: *This is the discontinuity that matters - not the change in structure but the change in philosophy.*

There is increasingly a consensus in the management literature that traditional models of analysing the structure of organisations are increasingly unsuitable. What is less often remarked is that non-hierarchical managerial systems have already evolved in many manufacturing organisations, although this may not always be apparent to the indigenous management (Brandon 1993).

Drucker (1989) suggests that future management systems will be based on structures like the British Raj, the Teaching Hospital and the Symphony Orchestra. In these organisations, instead of delegation of authority from the centre, each group of members in the organisation has a degree of intrinsic authority which derives from the recognition that they perform an essential task within the enterprise. The types of management structures advocated by Drucker can only be introduced if the principle of central control is sacrificed.

One of the most intractable problems in strategic change is that minor differences of meaning in our terminology may disguise assumptions concerning the structure of the organisation under analysis. The words of federalism are much softer than those of decentralisation: leadership rather than direction, consultation rather than instruction, etc. In a paper by Brandon et al. (1995) the transition from distributed production control to disseminated production management was proposed. The progression from *control* to *management* emphasises the differences between decentralised and federal structures of the organisation. The word *distributed,* again, implies direction from the centre whereas the authors noted that the meaning of the word *disseminated* is precise, but often has negative connotations, particularly the impossibility of maintaining centralised authority. (Concise Oxford Dictionary: *scatter about, sow in various places (esp. fig. of doctrines, sedition, disease, etc.)*).

References

J A Brandon, 1993, From the islands of automation to the knowledge archipelago: the challenge for manufacturing strategy in the 1990s, Proceedings of the Institution of Mechanical Engineers - Journal of Engineering Manufacture, **B207**, 141-146.

J A Brandon, M Troll and E Vollmer, 1995, From distributed production control to disseminated production management, Fifth International Conference on Flexible Automation and Integrated Manufacturing, (Editors, R D Scraft et al.), Stuttgart, Begell House, New York, 393-403.

C Handy, 1989, The age of unreason, Century Business Books, London.

Leo XIII, 1891,Papal Encyclical: Rerum novarum.

Pius XII, 1941, Papal Encyclical: Quadragesimo Anno.

M Porter, 1987 (May-June), From Competitive Advantage to Corporate Strategy, Harvard Business Review, 43-59.

E F Schumacher, 1973, Small is Beautiful: A Study of Economics as if People Mattered, Blond and Briggs, London.

Alfred P Sloan Jr., 1965, My years with General Motors, Sidgwick and Jackson, London.

THE HUMANISATION OF WORK: SOCIAL MOTIVATIONS FOR CELLULAR MANUFACTURING

The Hawthorne experiments demonstrated, if it were ever needed, that managerial control systems which focus exclusively on the productivity of the individual will be ineffective. As Miller and Form observed, work is a group activity and groups will evolve independently unless they are encouraged and stimulated by managerial initiatives.

The natural corollary of this observation is that there is scope to improve manufacturing effectiveness by reorganising production into self-managing teams. It is natural to match these teams to the production of a single product or a small range of products - a concept now popularly described as **ownership.**

By the early 1960s, research findings on the behaviour of working groups, for example by Eric Trist (Trist and Bamforth 1951) and Joan Woodward (1965), enabled the development of structured product-based teams. The work by Elliott Jacques (1951,1956), of the Tavistock Institute, and Wilfred Brown (1960), at the Glacier Metal Company, provided deep insights into the design of organisations in practice. Thus the managerial climate was receptive to organisational strategies based on group methods of working. A new form of cellular manufacturing, that of **Group Technology,** was consequently adopted with enthusiasm. The discussion here complements and amplifies an analysis of concurrent engineering and manufacturing (Brandon 1995).

The technical detail of Group Technology will be discussed later. The purpose of its introduction here is to record the discussions about the social context of introduction of an early form of cellular manufacturing system and assess whether Skinner's test of the managerial receptiveness of the organisation was satisfied.

Despite the insights provided by Skinner (1971), Edwards and Fazakerley (1974) suggest that the new form of cellular manufacturing was being analysed purely as a technological problem. As might be expected from Skinner's analysis, the prognosis for Group Technology was inauspicious. They observed that: *Too often the minor importance of the techniques has been overemphasized at the expense of the people they serve.*

Edwards and Fazakerley (1974) specified an extensive list of managerial factors which must be taken into account if the introduction of Group Technology is to be successful:

1. Existing functions and their current control

Although Group Technology was seen primarily as an activity in manufacturing, other functional groups would have to make significant changes in their own attitudes, behaviour and operational procedures. For example, sales and marketing departments might be required to provide more appropriate data to enable more realistic production forecasts.

The author has used the relationships between functional specialists in a Group Technology-based organisation to illustrate the requirements for successful implementation of **Concurrent Engineering,** a currently fashionable engineering methodology with much in common with Group Technology (Brandon 1995).

2. The position of works management

Few works managers are represented at senior levels. Even where works managers are present at the highest decision levels, there is commonly a mismatch of socio-economic background which inhibits communication. The author has argued that these considerations still apply and that the trend to corporate structures based on **Strategic Business Units (SBUs)** has accentuated the divisions (see Brandon 1992).

Subsequently, Leonard and Rathmill (1977), also based at Edwards's own institution (UMIST) but in Mechanical Engineering rather than

Management Sciences, published a paper which sealed the fate of Group Technology. Reading this paper again, nearly twenty years later, it is clear that these authors at least viewed the organisational issues from a traditional supervisory viewpoint.

3. Parochialism

Traditional rivalries between functional groups reduce the speed of change. However, Edwards and Fazakerley contend that *tramline thinking* is *not deliberate or planned* but rather a consequence of ingrained attitudes which have resulted from natural evolution of the functional organisation.

The author has suggested that traditional demarcations were a significant factor in the failure of the Group Technology movement in Britain in the 1970s (Brandon 1993,1995).

4. Fashions in management techniques

Associated with any new technological advance there will be a substantial proportion of companies who only introduce new methodologies or even only *pretend to introduce* them to *keep up with the 'Joneses'*.

As remarked by the author elsewhere, management exhibits the forms of the fashion but without any of the substance (Brandon 1992, pp160-161).

5. Difficulties of change in the production system

Changes in the production system are very difficult. Not only are such changes intrinsically difficult, but it is necessary to involve staff at different levels in the enterprise. Further, strategic change competes with essential operational issues in the priorities of production management.

6. *Resistors*

Change itself threatens the position and security of staff. Often they are only able to influence events whilst they are able to maintain the *status quo*.

 As remarked by the author (Brandon 1988), those under the strongest threat have the strongest vested interest in minimising the benefits of new organisational methodologies and maximising the potential costs. Later studies, for example by Scase and Goffee (1984), suggest that middle managers who see their position and/or tenure threatened may be the most reluctant to commit themselves to change.

Caldwell (1993) suggests *six steps to success* in communication of change to employees:

* *Clarify goals;*

At first sight this requirement seems patronising - would a company really embark on a programme of radical technological and managerial change without a clearly articulated set of goals? Regrettably, the answer is usually yes. Parkinson and Rowe (1977, Chapter 11) suggest that the explanation why many organisations fail to set communication objectives is that, in order to define how to reach some future destination, one has to have a reasonable idea of one's current position! They remark: *Most companies just guess at this, and usually guess wrong.*

Obviously, goals should be refined and adjusted, as the change programme progresses, but it is essential to have a coherent communications strategy from the outset. Further, communication is an integral - indeed central - part of the change process.

- *Identify audiences;*

  Different groups have a variety of perceptions, concerns, expectations and attitudes. Each will see different threats and opportunities in change programmes. As Caldwell observes, in talking about a new job evaluation and grading scheme: *[it] may have the effect of creating a large group of perceived losers, when in fact there are only a small group of real losers.*

- *Assess resistance;*

  Although change is a natural process, both inevitable and desirable, it is common for employees to view it with suspicion and trepidation. Caldwell suggests that resistance to change can be classified into four categories:

  - *Defensive self-interest;*
  - *Lack of trust;*
  - *Different assessments;*
  - *Anxiety.*

  Each of these forms of resistance is a response to a different stimulus. Each must be addressed separately For example, lack of trust will originate from a perception of previous broken promises. Different assessments may be due to misunderstandings about the implications of the change strategy - once again evidence of failures in communication.

Caldwell implies that loss of support of *critical constituencies* can be fatal to change strategies. He further contends that some resistance to change is inevitable and that well-thought-out management strategies for building support for change are essential.

- *Put the message across;*

In many organisations there is an implicit assumption that the despatch of a communication is equivalent to its receipt. Reliance is placed on the traditional rules that messages should be limited in number, simple in structure and regularly repeated. Realistically, where the messages are intended to bring about changes in the structure of the organisation itself, a message must thread a path through an organisational minefield. For example, Caldwell suggests that instructions may be interpreted as advice because of a natural inclination on the part of the superior to avoid being regarded as unduly assertive. In traditional organisations with a tall hierarchy, inaccuracies will accrue simply because of the number of times a message is transmitted.

Caldwell advocates *careful pruning of the organisational structure.* In the introduction of cellular manufacturing systems, however, the re-design of the organisational structure itself is implicit in the change.

Perhaps more difficult to address, but more important in the context of radical change, is the vulnerability of messages to suppression or deliberate distortion by those who regard the planned changes as threats. Such staff must be identified and either convinced of the desirability of the change programme or their ability to disrupt the change eliminated.

Caldwell refers to staff with power to influence events in this way as *gatekeepers.* Taylor (1986) defines gatekeepers in the following terms: *Gatekeepers, or 'special communicators', have access to more and better information than their colleagues and they more readily communicate that information.*

- ### *Train communicators;*

   It is evident that changes in management structure require re-definition of roles within the organisation. Nowhere is this more significant than in communication where it is necessary to change from control by instruction to communication by means of advocacy. Caldwell remarks that *commitment* must be encouraged rather than *compliance* and *participation* rather than *control.*

- ### *Media choices.*

   In the light of the foregoing discussion, the option of propagating information though such media as *newsletters, brochures and videos* seems appropriate. Everyone in the organisation receives the same information simultaneously. Opportunities for confusion, rivalry and misinterpretation are minimised. Caldwell rejects this argument as a *'quick-fix' solution.* He contrasts the *preference for media rather than dialogue,* which trivialises communication, turning it into a budgetary problem rather than one of managerial communication.

   In conclusion, Caldwell notes that good communication cannot in itself guarantee successful change management, since it cannot compensate for a defective strategy; bad communication can, however, destroy an otherwise excellent programme of change.

7. Traditional attitudes

As with the experience of Frederick Taylor, Edwards and Fazakerley note that the knowledge and experience built up through long service in an organisation is invaluable under steady-state operating conditions but can be a severe disadvantage under conditions of radical change.

Return on investment, meeting delivery dates, the levels of absenteeism and throughput are suitable indicators of effectiveness for assessing performance under cellular manufacturing organisation.

8. Product orientation

As Edwards and Fazakerley remark, the long history of organisational stability in many industries leads to a preference for the *status quo*. It is surprising to find that they suggest that this is a product-focused culture. They are quite right to observe, however, that change agents must be constantly aware of the strength of the prevailing cultural values, choosing carefully when to disregard the consequences of established values and when to respect them.

9. Information level prior to change

Much of the data required for system design is either of poor quality or simply not recorded. The problem may not only be to select the best of conflicting data but rather to decide which people will be able to provide valuable data which is only recorded in their own memories.

10. Education

Although this is usually one of the most neglected areas in planning strategic change, Edwards and Fazakerley devote more space to this issue than to any other topic.

As with other systems of cellular manufacturing, and also with more general innovations such as concurrent engineering, the impact of the changes on functional groups outside manufacturing must be identified, quantified and communicated to those affected. The emphasis is, quite rightly, on explanation, advocacy and obtaining consent.

11. Trade unions

The implicit changes in introducing group working practices involve many of the issues which have traditionally led to industrial strife. They suggest, however, that in a number of applications the reality was substantially less difficult than the expectation. There is perhaps an implicit suggestion, when taken with the other issues, that trade unions will participate positively in introducing new technologies provided they perceive an overall benefit to their members.

12. Time

As with all radical innovations, the time to introduce group methods of working can easily be underestimated. Edwards and Fazakerley list:

Time for thought,

time for planning,

time for training,

time for working together in new ways with new people with different skill patterns, and

time for entering into and hearing about other people's problems.

It has often been observed that time is always available to make endless poorly planned and abortive attempts at an innovation but never enough time to carry it out once properly. It must be emphasised that benefits of careful planning and constant awareness of the overall aim of the programme are key factors in minimising the overall timescales for project implementation.

13.   *Financial considerations*

As with all programmes of strategic change, the transition to new methods of organisation is fated to be measured according to traditional financial performance measures. Edwards and Fazakerley observe that this seems, at first sight, *reasonable and capable of receiving a quick and sensible answer.* They contend, however, that such simple quantitative measures cannot estimate realistically the benefits (or the costs) to the whole system. They suggest that the change agent must utilise a wide range of management ratios to evaluate the benefits of the change.

In many respects the findings of Edwards and Fazakerley are far from novel; they have been presented before and since. What is remarkable, however, is the apparent paradox that their research was widely quoted (in particular Edwards's *Readings in Group Technology 1971)* - and presumably widely read - but seems to have been largely disregarded in practice. Their practical experience will be considered again when the technical aspects of Group Technology are discussed.

Writing independently, Fazakerley (1974) applied criteria from the social sciences to construct a framework for developing the social structures suitable for group-based production systems. She noted the irony that the innovations of Scientific Management had, for the first time, created a need for literacy amongst production operatives, to read process layouts and machining charts. Simultaneously, *white collar* occupations had been created to perform the indirect activities of Scientific Management, for example the creation of those same process layouts and machining charts. She argued that the educational system then *develops its own momentum.* (To attribute this to the work of Taylor and Gilbreth does something of a disservice to industrial training movements in Europe in the nineteenth century, for example the founding of the Mechanics' Institutes in Britain mainly in the second quarter of the century - Carter and Williams 1957.)

Unfortunately, for industrial competitiveness at least, education stimulates dissatisfactions with manual work. The removal of control over work, because of the external analysis of job content, also leads to dissatisfaction. Fazakerley noted that symptoms of dissatisfaction - *job alienation, absenteeism, labour turnover and poor industrial relations* - were less prevalent in batch manufacture than in mass production. She questioned whether the discontent already apparent in mass production would, in time, become a feature in batch production. She observed that batch manufacture accounted for some eighty percent. of manufacturing organisations and that any such problems would have major social and economic impact.

Fazakerley argued that the *value of group technology lies in part in [a] combination of technical and social factors* - once again justifying their evaluation against Skinner's criterion. She observed that the removal of frustration due to the broader scope of jobs in group technology would increase motivation and could be a significant factor in the removal of social problems She commented that the fashionable preoccupation with *job enrichment* schemes was probably potentially far less rewarding, though probably more interesting to managers, than systematically identifying and removing sources of frustration.

In many respects the job enrichment is important, but its implementation must be consistent with the industrial context. Fazakerley observes that group-based working changes the roles both of direct workers and their supervisors. Devolution of control over a sequence of production operations on a family of components: *not only establishes responsibility for quality and quantity but also lays the basis for pride in accomplishment.* It is natural that the group assume a willingness to solve technical problems which previously would have been outside their control and, consequently, of minimal concern. With the changes in operators' responsibilities, the supervisor is able to take a more positive and strategic role.

Effects on managerial roles outside the production function are less evident immediately but no less radical and potentially beneficial. As Fazakerley observes, these may follow a *period of unsettling self-concern.*

Fazakerley notes that the changes of function may be subtle and the transition accompanied by *ambiguities and inconsistencies.* As does Caldwell (1993), she emphasises the importance of *full and honest communication.* Both the purpose of the change and its implications must be frankly presented - insofar as they are known - all programmes of change have unexpected consequences, sometimes beneficial but perhaps more often deleterious. She suggests that one essential function of external change agents is to relieve affected managers of their day-to-day concerns so that they may concentrate on the process of change.

Fazakerley suggests that similar concerns amongst production operatives and their supervisors may be disguised behind concerns about de-skilling or loss of status. Recall Miller and Form's fourth principle, derived from that: *a complaint may reflect insecurity of status rather than an objective response to events.* Whilst craft personnel may experience some temporary loss of self-esteem due to elimination of a specialist job specification, turner, miller, etc., this may become a source of peer esteem in a multi-skilled group even though the specialist may be expected to perform operations outside the narrow confines of the original craft. She contends that craft specialists, with their high levels of skill and experience, are less likely to be expected to participate in flexible manning arrangements than the published literature would suggest.

Edwards and Fazakerley were participants in what is probably the most extensive programme of academic-industry co-operation organised in Britain. It involved five universities and sixty-seven industrial companies. The official record of this programme, sponsored by the British Science Research Council, was collated by John Burbidge (1979a). Although Schonberger (1990) credits the invention of Group Technology to the Russian researchers, he describes the British programme as a *Crucible of Cellular Thought.*

Schonberger singles out five individuals who participated in the British programme for particular mention. Of these Burbidge and Edwards were academics, Gordon Ransom and Charles Allen were industrial managers, and Joseph Gombinski was an independent consultant.

Following on from his involvement in the British research, Burbidge undertook an international study at the International Centre for Advanced Technical and Vocational Training in Turin (Burbidge 1976, 1979b). In many respects this work had a wider scope, in that the focus was intended to be on the **humanisation of work** rather than on any specific strategy to attain that aim. As might be expected, however, Burbidge's research was coloured by his earlier experience with Group Technology.

The primary motivation for the programme was what Burbidge described as *the concept of humanisation of work.* It was based on three *premises:*

- Work should be natural and satisfying;
- The planning and organisation of work affects job satisfaction;
- That prevailing methods of work organisation preclude job satisfaction.

The deficiencies of prevailing methods of work organisation were:

- Simple, repetitive, short cycle tasks;
- Removal of discretion from the worker by means of external job design;
- Imposition of a fixed-cycle working pace - by machines or conveyors;
- Forms of organisation which preclude formation of group identities;
- Jobs designed for the convenience of the machine rather than the comfort of the operative;
- Jobs are determined by processes rather than products - eliminates sense of creating a useful artefact.

The scope of **humanisation of work** encompassed six areas of managerial concern:

- Job design;
- Production organisation;

- Participation;

- Training and staff development;

- Ergonomics;

- Working conditions.

Burbidge noted that the programme shared these attributes with the ideas of **Socio-technological Systems**, developed at the Tavistock Institute, and the **Quality of Work programme,** in the USA. He related **humanisation of work** to these conceptual frameworks and other topical ideas in industrial sociology, as shown.

As has been mentioned, Burbidge approached the humanisation of work from his background in Production Management and in particular group production. The emphasis of the humanisation of work programme was influenced accordingly. For example, there is very little attention given to working conditions because *their feasibility and effectiveness are not affected by the introduction of group production methods.* Thus, implicitly, Burbidge discounted the - probably not inconsiderable - contributions of improvement of working conditions to the humanisation of work. To address the issue of job design, Burbidge advocated the systematic increasing of task content, cycle time and variety of task.

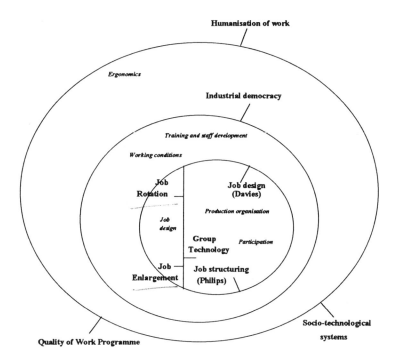

Relationships between Burbidge's Humanisation of Work study and other contemporary social concepts (After Burbidge 1979b: Figure 2/2).

Production organisation - perhaps predictably - is improved according to the *premise that people have a need to belong to goal-seeking-groups.* A natural solution is one based on product- based groups rather than production organisation arranged according to process needs. In an extensive survey by Ingersoll (1990), 77% of respondents reported using product-based cells, 58% used process-based cells, and 35% were using a mix of process- and product-based cells.

Burbidge distinguished between more general methods for increasing participation at work, for example through greater representation in the management of the company, and the more local delegation of decision making to groups of workers on the shop-floor. The programme was concerned only with the latter issue.

Burbidge's treatment of training and education, and ergonomics, is uncontroversial. What is, perhaps, unusual is the apparent failure to recognise this as a leading priority in the success of organisational change (Ingersoll 1990, Wille 1992, Hörnell 1992).

The outcome of the study was expressed in eight conclusions, which Burbidge describes as *hypotheses which still need further testing*:

- *General*: Group production requires an organisational change from process-based systems to product-based groups.

- *Job satisfaction*: Evidence of improved job satisfaction was judged to be positive but subjective, largely due to the difficulty in defining an objective test of job satisfaction.

- *Economic effects*: Economic gains were due to reduced costs and reduction in inventory costs.

- *Technological limitations*: Although there is no apparent limit to the applicability of group-based production methods, there may be some industries where technological design requirements inhibit group working.

- *Shop-floor participation*: Effective delegation of decisions is more feasible in group-based production systems.

- *Methods of introduction of group production methods*: Burbidge contends that the more successful applications are those which have gained the commitment and leadership of senior executives of the company. He suggests that incremental introduction of group-based production - one group at a time - tends to breed opposition.

- *Time taken*: Burbidge suggests a period of at least two years as a reasonable planning estimate for such a radical innovation.

- *Disadvantages*: Burbidge cites possible redundancies and reduction in promotion opportunities as the principal disadvantages.

The description of these as hypotheses rather than conclusions has much to recommend it. In many ways they reflect the preconceptions Burbidge took into the study rather than an objective interpretation of the evidence. Perhaps it would be most accurate to describe them as Burbidge's convictions.

The formation of workers into groups is achievable in process-based systems, although it may be more of a challenge. That group working is a natural feature in process-based organisations had been established in the Hawthorne experiments (Gillespie 1991). In apparent disregard for fashionable ideas about lean production (Womack et al. 1990), in 1995 Toyota implemented a classical assembly-line system for their RAV4 four-wheel-drive vehicle but redesigned, with reduced automation, to give assembly operatives control of the rate of flow (Anon. 1995). This is achieved by allowing (small) buffer stocks between production units (cells?), once again flying in the face of the received wisdom of lean production. As *The Economist* observes: ***To switch from machines to people looks a strange strategy - particularly given Japan's astronomical labour costs.*** Toyota point to substantial savings due to reductions in indirect staff costs in the maintenance function and significantly lower investment costs, when compared to their highly automated factories elsewhere. As an intangible benefit they suggest that reducing dependence on relatively inflexible automation in the assembly line increases opportunities for *Kaizen* - the quest for continuous improvement (Imai 1986).

It is probably fair to say that the enhancement of job satisfaction was not Burbidge's first priority. Nor did he pay any great attention to the role of technology in Group Technology. Burbidge was primarily preoccupied with effectiveness and efficiency of production management. He saw the route to prosperity - and indirectly to job satisfaction - through the simplification of the flow of material through the factory. As Fazakerley (1974) had observed, externally stimulated programmes of job enrichment are unlikely to succeed where frustration with lack of control of the operating environment prevails. Thus Burbidge's methods are likely to improve job satisfaction as a secondary effect rather than a primary motivation.

Leonard and Rathmill (1977) questioned the claims made for improvement in job satisfaction under Group Technology organisational principles. They echoed Burbidge's doubts whether there was an objective measure of job satisfaction, particularly when observers do not compare like with like. They observed that Group Technology implementations - which necessarily had been the subject of sustained managerial effort - were being compared with typical flow-line systems which had never undergone the same level of intensive analysis and intervention. They contended that the effectiveness of Group Technology could only be judged in comparison with functional layout systems which had received the same managerial attention.

The issues of economic effects and technological limitations will not be discussed here, not because they are unimportant but rather because of their marginal relevance to the social motivation for introducing Group Technology.

Shop-floor participation is one of the few essential features of Group Technology - and other forms of group working - that all commentators agree about. In many respects this is obvious - without their co-operation and participation it is impossible to organise workers into groups! Similarly, it is difficult to envisage a radical culture change in any organisation without the leadership of its senior management - although it is increasingly common for the changes to be initiated from below (Waterlow and Monniot 1986).

On the issue of incremental introduction of culture change, the consensus of experience tends to contradict that of Burbidge. Considerable value has been placed on building the experience from one project in group methods of working into subsequent projects (see, for example, Gill 1986). As Caldwell (1993) remarked, overcoming resistance to change is an implicit task of management in any change in the structure of the enterprise. Morone (1989) observes: *Successful new products and processes emerge gradually, over the source of a sequence of earlier product and process introductions.* Burbidge's recommendation would now be described as *betting the company;* it certainly demonstrates the commitment of senior management but - in most cases - would be regarded as a reckless risk. Ingersoll Engineers (1990) advocated the use of *pilot schemes to generate confidence and experience.* Their opinion must carry considerable weight since Ingersoll have been strongly identified with cellular manufacturing systems for over twenty years (NEDO 1975).

Similarly, the constant re-appraisal of staffing numbers and review of roles are the responsibility of corporate management. It is not by any means an aspect specific to Group Technology, although it may well consume a considerable amount of management effort.

The period of two years suggested by Burbidge would probably be regarded now as a relatively short time to introduce a radical change in the culture of an organisation. It is probably a reasonable estimate of the period necessary to introduce the mechanisms of organisation, but the values will require constant reinforcement over much more prolonged periods.

References

Anon., 1995 (March 24th), The kindergarten that will change the world, The Economist, 81-82.

J A Brandon, 1988, Where Consultants Fall Down, Management Today, 109-119.

J A Brandon, 1992, Structural impediments to strategic change in the technological enterprise, Journal of Strategic Change, 1(6), 333-339.

J A Brandon, 1993, On the vulnerability of programmes of strategic change to functional interests: a case study, Journal of Strategic Change, 2(3), 151-156.

J A Brandon, 1995, Concurrent engineering and manufacturing infrastructure, Fifth International Conference on Flexible Automation and Integrated Manufacturing, Stuttgart (Editors, R D Schraft et al.), Begell House, New York, 1124-1133.

W Brown, 1960, Exploration in Management: A description of the Glacier Metal Company's concepts and methods of organisation and management, Heinemann, London.

J L Burbidge, 1976, Group production methods and the humanisation of work: the evidence in industrialised countries, Research Series #10, International Centre for Advanced Technical and Vocational Training, Turin.

J L Burbidge, 1979a, Group Technology in the Engineering Industry, Mechanical Engineering Publications, Bury St Edmunds.

J L Burbidge, 1979b, A study of the effects of group production methods on the humanisation of work, Final report: International Centre for Advanced Technical and Vocational Training, Turin.

R Caldwell, 1993, Is anyone listening? Communicating change to employees, Journal of Strategic Change, 2(2), 83-87.

C F Carter and B R Williams, 1957, Industry and Technical Progress: Factors Influencing the Speed and Application of Science, Oxford University Press, England.

G A B Edwards, 1971, Readings in Group Technology, Machinery Publishing Company, Brighton, England.

G A B Edwards and G M Fazakerley, 1973, The cell system of production embraces group technology and also concerns management, technical and social change, Proceedings of the 14th Machine Tool Design and Research Conference (Editors, F Koenigsberger and S Tobias), Manchester, 197-206.

G M Fazakerley, 1974, Group technology: social benefits and social problems, The Production Engineer, 383-386.

R E Flanders, 1924, Design, Manufacture, and Production Control of a Standard Machine, Transactions of the American Society of Mechanical Engineers, 46, 691-738.

R Gillespie, 1993, Manufacturing Knowledge: A history of the Hawthorne experiments, Cambridge University Press, Cambridge, England.

E Hörnell, 1992, Improving productivity for competitive advantage: Lessons from the best in the world, Pitman, London.

M Imai, 1986, Kaizen: The key to Japan's competitive success, Random House, New York.

Ingersoll Engineers, 1990, Competitive Manufacturing: The quiet revolution, Ingersoll Engineers, Rugby, England.

E Jacques, 1951, The Changing Culture of a Factory, Tavistock Publications, London/ Dryden Press, New York.

E Jacques, 1956, Measurement of Responsibility, Tavistock Publications, London/ Harvard University Press, Cambridge, Ma.

C N Parkinson and N Rowe, 1977, Communicate: Parkinson's Formula for Business Survival, Prentice-Hall, London.

R Leonard and K Rathmill, 1977 (January), The Group Technology myths, Management Today, 66-69.

J Morone, 1989 (Summer), Strategic use of technology, California Management Review, 91- 110.

NEDO, 1975, Why Group Technology? National Economic Development Office, London.

W Skinner, 1971 (January-February), The Anachronistic Factory, Harvard Business Review, 61-70.

E L Trist and K W Bamforth ,1951, Some social and psychological consequences of the longwall method of coal-getting, Human Relations, 4 (1) 6-24 and 37-8 (reprinted in D S Pugh, 1971 Organization Theory, Penguin, Harmondsworth, 345-369).

R Scase and R Goffee, 1984, Reluctant Managers: Their Work and Lifestyles, Unwin-Hyman, London.

R J Schonberger, 1990, Building a Chain of Customers: Linking Business Functions to Create the World Class Company, Hutchinson Business Books, London.

R L Taylor, 1986, The impact of organisational change on the technological gatekeeper role, IEEE Transactions on Engineering Management, EM-33(1), 12-16.

J G Waterlow and J P Monniot, 1986, A study of the state-of-the-art in computer-aided production management in UK industry, ACME Directorate, Science and Engineering Research Council, Swindon, England.

E Wille, 1992, Quality: Achieving excellence, Century Business, London.

J P Womack, D T Jones and D Roos, 1990, The machine that changed the world, Rawson Associates, New York.

J Woodward, 1965, Industrial Organisation: Theory and Practice, Oxford University Press, Oxford (N.B. later editions exist).

ELEMENTARY ENGINEERING ECONOMICS: ECONOMIC BATCH QUANTITY

Like many measures in manufacturing systems, the **Economic Batch Quantity (EBQ)** is invaluable as a qualitative indicator but virtually useless as a planning aid. Here, the analysis of Hicks (1994) is used to illustrate the use and usefulness of the measure although the relevant analysis is presented in the overwhelming majority of texts on manufacturing systems.

Two forms of the EBQ are commonly used in manufacturing management: The first, **Economic Order Quantity (EOQ)**, is *".. [a] compromise between the sum of the costs associated with order preparation and inventory holding .."* (Hicks 1994) and is essentially external to the activities of manufacturing engineering. The alternative, **Economic Production Quantity (EPQ)**, depends on parameters within the control of manufacturing engineers *".. production control often has an analogous sum-of-costs problem with machine lot sizes that determine machine setup cost and WIP (work-in-process) inventory holding cost."* (ibid.)

For EOQ, Hicks derives the formula:

$$Q_o = \sqrt{\frac{2PA}{H}}$$

84

Where

Qo = Economic order quantity
P   = Cost of placing an order
A   = Annual usage rate
H   = Annual unit holding cost

This formula, quite properly, requires staff within the procurement function to evaluate and issue order quantities based on variables within their knowledge or control.

For EPQ, used within the production function, Hicks derives a formula based on the variables within the knowledge or control of manufacturing engineers:

$$Q_o = \sqrt{\frac{2SA}{H(1-D/P)}}$$

Where

Qo = economic production quantity
S = Set-up cost
A = Annual usage rate
H = Annual unit holding cost
D = Daily usage rate
P = Daily production rate

Although the formula has the same structure, the variables differ and, confusingly, the significance of the variable P has changed. This is of little direct consequence in a business where all management is functionalised, but it is indicative of potential conflicts between staff using different measures of performance for optimising interacting systems. Hicks observes:

It should be noted that EOQ and EPQ are important today not so much as a means to setting operating policy but as a means to gaining a basic understanding of underlying relationships between certain inventory control costs.

It would be reassuring to believe that this were so. In many companies, however, batch size or reorder formulae are still used as a central feature of the production planning process. It is instructive, therefore, to consider how the two measures interact.

Firstly, take the case where the EOQ is substantially greater than the EBQ. An order for the EOQ will be issued from the procurement function. In production planning this order will be segmented into a number of batches, each of which will be scheduled independently, each corresponding to the EBQ. Conversely, if the EBQ is much greater than the EOQ, production planning will retain a number of orders until an economic production quantity is attained. Where EOQ and EBQ are of similar scale, it is likely that production planners will respond according to their perception of priorities and expediencies. If the shop-floor is slack they will choose the larger number and if it is congested the smaller.

In multi-stage batch manufacturing, EBQ will vary from machine to machine because each will have different setup costs and production rates. If applied strictly, the EBQ approach requires orders to be re-batched between operations. This is by no means unusual in batch manufacturing.

The effort required in the collection of the data to compute EBQs is far from trivial. Often the EBQ for a product/machine combination is based on operating conditions observed at best in the last annual stocktaking exercise but more commonly a long time previously. It is by no means unusual to find production planners using estimates of EBQ based on long-discredited values of usage rate, setup time, holding cost, etc. Further, inaccuracies in the EBQ are likely to be self-reinforcing: if the computed cost is too high then demand is likely to fall thereby aggravating the perceived excess costs due to low demand.

Burbidge (1972, p.75) summarised the deficiencies of fixed-batch/order-quantity production control systems:

- *High investment in stocks*
- *Variable and unpredictable changes in both work-in-progress and finished stock*
- *Variable and unpredictable load on machines*
- *It is impossible to realise savings from "family processing"*
- *Variations in demand are magnified at each succeeding inventory stage*
- *Material obsolescence*
- *Unreliable under conditions of varying demand.*

Latterly, Burbidge (1986,1989) advocated an alternative system of production control - **Period Batch Control** - which allows variable batch quantities but fixes the reorder interval. This simplifies the process of production scheduling at the cost of manufacturing with batch quantities which deviate from the theoretical optimum. Since the data used in deriving the EBQ values are often of dubious validity, and usually outdated, there is considerable merit in Burbidge's arguments.

It is now widely acknowledged among management accountants that manufacturing cost systems have distorted the operational strategy of many organisations (Kaplan 1984). Johnson and Kaplan (1987) reported that more realistic costing systems were available in the early years of the twentieth century but were gradually displaced because of the prohibitive cost of maintaining them with manual clerical systems. With the availability of virtually unlimited computer power, such costing systems are in the process of re-establishment (Innes et al. 1994).

Although it is important to realise that traditional measures such as EOQ and EBQ continue to be used widely in batch manufacturing, the purpose of the analysis presented here is in keeping with the view quoted from Hicks, above, to acquire an understanding of the relationships between the cost drivers in batch manufacturing.

The formula for EBQ quoted from Hicks involves (amongst other variables) a ratio between two cost elements, the setup cost of the machine, S, and the holding cost, **H**.

There is considerable merit in considering the implications of these cost elements in the wider management context. Both are representative of inefficiencies in production.

Setup costs represent unproductive machine time. The formula indicates that batch sizes may be reduced if setup costs are minimised. As will be seen, there are several ways of attacking setup costs which lead to different forms of cellular manufacturing systems, for example:

- Retaining existing manufacturing technology and re-organising the flow of work, for example so that components which have similar setups are scheduled sequentially;

- Introduction of flexible machines;

- Introducing new manufacturing technology with intrinsically simpler setup, for example by palletising components rather than on-machine fixturing.

In the third category, it is well known, for example, that Taiichi Ohno, developer of the Toyota Production System, set the achievement of **Single Minute Exchange of Dies (SMED)** as a central objective of the system (Shingo 1981).

Turning now to annual holding costs: if these are low then, on the basis of the EBQ formula, large batch sizes can be tolerated. Since many manufacturers have historically had little or no basis on which to assign holding costs, their validity is difficult to estimate. Tangibly, raw materials, (much of the) work-in-progress and finished stocks are non-performing assets: their value can, at least, be multiplied by the target rate of return to give an opportunity cost. Tangibly, they occupy a substantial proportion of space in the factory, which costs a rental, once again a computable opportunity cost. Intangibly, there are substantial costs due to congestion and confusion on the shop-floor. Costs of obsolescence, unreported quality problems and degradation are easily concealed and are rarely assessed. (They would probably be too embarrassing for many companies.) Instead, they are aggregated into an inexorably increasing general overhead.

Taking the view that any out-of-process artefact represents a non-performing asset, it is easy to see the logic of Taiichi Ohno that all production operations should work on a **Just-in-Time (JIT)** basis (Shinohara 1985). If inventory is eliminated then so are the tangible aspects of holding costs; so also are the intangible costs.

References

J L Burbidge, 1972, The case for flow control/ Inventory planning and control, Chapters 5 and 6 *in* Managing Materials in Industry (Editors, P Baily and D Farmer), Gower Press, London, 62-94.

J L Burbidge, 1986, A future for the engineering industry, International Conference, Engineering Management: Theory and Applications, Swansea, M Jackson, Redruth, England, 141-149.

J L Burbidge, 1989, Group Technology, Chapter 21 *in* International Handbook of Production and Operations Management, (Editor, R Wild), Cassell, London, 384-401.

P E Hicks, 1994, Industrial Engineering and Management: A New Perspective, McGraw-Hill, New York.

J Innes, F Mitchell and T Yoshikawa, 1994, Activity Costing for Engineers, Research Studies Press, Taunton.

H T Johnson and R S Kaplan, 1987, Relevance Lost: The Rise and Fall of Management Accounting, Harvard Business School Press, Boston, Ma.

R S Kaplan, 1984 (July-August), Yesterday's accounting undermines production, Harvard Business Review, 95-101.

S Shingo, 1981, Study of 'Toyota' Production System from Industrial Engineering Viewpoint, Japan Management Association, Tokyo.

I Shinohara, 1985, NPS New Production System: Crossing Industrial Boundaries, Toyo Keizai Shinposha, Tokyo.

A SIMPLE QUANTITATIVE METHOD FOR CLASSIFYING THE STRUCTURE OF MANUFACTURING SYSTEMS

It is a good principle in manufacturing that models should be simple without being simplistic; indeed this is a re-statement of the classical philosophical principle known as **Occam's razor**. Unfortunately it is a principle more evident by its absence than by its observance. All too often, quantitative methods are too complex and qualitative methods are too superficial.

An ideal model is one where useful information is provided by a single statistic. A valuable indicator of the ideal structure of a manufacturing system is provided by **Hitomi's P:Q ratio** (Hitomi 1990).

	Production Quantity **Low**	**Q** **High**
Product Variety P **Low**	**Depending on prevailing attitudes and practices**	**Product-based layout**
High	**Process-based layout**	**Depending on prevailing attitudes and practices**

The number of products is given by the variable **P**; the total production quantity is **Q**. The natural structure of production layout can be determined from the table. For low volumes and high variety (low P:Q ratio), there is little justification for specialising the production layout to individual products. Conversely, for high volumes with minimal variety there is considerable value in designing manufacturing layout around the optimal needs of the product.

The other two cases depend largely on context. System design will be dominated by the history of the organisation and, where strategic planning is undertaken, on the projections of its future.

In *evolving* manufacturing systems it is most likely that a system with a future in high volume - high variety has developed from an organisation with lower volumes but similar variety. (It would be relatively unusual for a manufacturer to seek to broaden the range in an existing high-volume system.) Because of this preferential process of evolution, it is most likely that high-volume - high-variety (intermediate P:Q) would continue to be a process-based type of manufacturing system (from origins as low P:Q).

As with Taylor's experience of introduction of high-speed steel, proposals for new methods of organisation of production must take into account the long history of familiarity with tried and trusted methods. They must also be sensitive to attitudes to the received viewpoints of the alternative technologies. As Fazakerley (1974) remarked, the public perception of mass-production techniques (high P:Q) was far from favourable. The solution adopted by a number of companies, Group Technology, had the significant advantage that high variety was perceived by the customer at the same time that changes in production organisation were improved internally to lower effective variety and increase volumes. For example, recognition that two batches of components can utilise the same set up halves the P:Q ratio, eliminates half of the set-up costs, whilst maintaining the customer's perception of product differentiation.

Once the decision is made that the P:Q ratio is sufficiently high that a product-based layout would be advantageous, attitudes to a wide variety of production-engineering issues change. These affect:

- machine design - machines may be task-specific and purpose-built;

- training - the skills are now vested in the machine rather than the operator (Alford's third law - Alford 1940);

- inventory management - now mechanistic, since it is simplified due to reduced variety of product;

- materials handling - may be customised to the product (or small range of products);

- sequential coupling of production operations - batches are scheduled simultaneously through a sequence of processes, eliminating much of the need for inter-operation storage.

References

L P Alford, 1940, Principles of Industrial Management, The Ronald Press, New York.
G M Fazakerley, 1974, Group technology: social benefits and social problems, The Production Engineer, 383-386.
K Hitomi, Manufacturing systems engineering: the concept, its context and the state of the art, International Journal of Computer Integrated Manufacture, 3(5), 1990, 275-288.

THE LIMITATIONS OF FUNCTIONAL LAYOUT

Many of the researchers whose work has been reviewed here take the case for product-based organisation of manufacturing as obvious and irrefutable. This overwhelming confidence in the new methods of production organisation was, paradoxically, one of the inhibiting features in the adoption of product based systems. This is, perhaps, not surprising; functional layout was the system with which most manufacturing engineers were most familiar and in which they had the confidence of many years of evolutionary development. The work of Taylor had created the impression that the organisational problems of process-based systems had either been solved or were unsolvable. The traumas of the introduction of Scientific Management were remembered and could be expected all over again if radically different systems of manufacturing organisation were to be adopted.

As Gallagher (1983) observed, the description of the layout of Stephenson's locomotive factory of 1844 would - for most purposes - have served perfectly adequately nearly one hundred and thirty years later. Many of the original justifications for that layout - for example the necessity to arrange machines of similar load-speed characteristics together, to take power from a common line-shaft - were no longer applicable. The line-shaft had given way to independent electrical drives for each of the machine tools. Thus, as is common in organisations, the practice perpetuated after the reasons for its adoption became irrelevant.

Gallagher (1983) analysed the strengths and weaknesses of functional layout:

94

Strengths	Weaknesses
Flexibility	Poor materials handling
A wide range of products can be produced	The variety of products inhibits introduction of materials-handling equipment
General-purpose equipment	Long through-put times
Enables change of product variants	although individual batch production times may only aggregate to a few hours, components may be in the factory for months
Less vulnerable to changes in demand mix	
Lower investment	Complex scheduling
Ability to segregate dirty, noisy or dangerous operations	Complex cost accounting

Gallagher remarked that functionally based manufacturing systems had evolved gradually. He observed that it is easy to underestimate the comparative differences in organisational complexity as a factory grows in size. He contrasts the differences between an original factory of thirty machines and fifty workers and one with three hundred machines and five hundred workers. The same methods of control are, however, applied to both.

Implicit in the work of Williamson (1968) is that the interaction between the organisation of batch manufacture and the design of machine tools is mutually reinforcing. The organisation of the factory reflected existing social structures, encapsulating the specialisation of the group. If the group itself had a narrow range of craft skills then it is logical that new machines provided for their use should be specialised to those skills. Thus the new machines were tailored to their anticipated usage. Williamson contended that: *.. as the invention of a new product gave rise to a demand, the technology and organisation of manufacture were evolved together to meet and further stimulate the demand.*

Gallagher refers to the influential study by Hollier (1964) for accurate characterisation of production control in manufacturing. It is, perhaps, surprising to find Gallagher having to rely on a study already nearly twenty years old, but there are in fact very few detailed case studies. Much of the published research data relies on survey data.

Penn (1994) observes that there are two *styles of contemporary research in Britain concerning the relationship of technical change and work organisation.* The first, based on surveys, meets few of the sociologist's criteria of validity. Penn comments on their dependence on *descriptive data;* describes them as *a-theoretical and a-historical;* and suggests that their motivation as *policy-driven research* compromises their validity as *mainstream sociological enquiry.* The second form of research - typified by the *Labour Process Conferences - .... finds little difficulty in generalizing* and *... much of the research recorded in these books is cavalier in its treatment of data and often merely anecdotal.*

It is hardly surprising that none of Schonberger's five visionaries of Cellular Manufacturing (Schonberger 1990) gains a mention in the research treatise of Penn et al. (1994) on *Skill and Occupational Change*, despite the irony that one of the editors (Rubery) teaches in the same establishment - Manchester School of Management, UMIST - where Edwards and Fazakerley did their pioneering investigations.

This discomfort with writers and thinkers who disregard the scientific conventions of social research is evident in the work of Burns and Stalker (1994). They invest in Weber - *the founder of the study of bureaucracy* - a *set of principles* [which] *underlie every subsequent definition given to formal organisation in industry; they can even be read, in garbled form, in Henri Fayol's principles of management ....* They describe Fayol's definitions of management and organisation as *.. no more than a thesaurus of* *synonyms.* Sportingly, Burns and Stalker suggest that Fayol may not have been aware of the rigorous analysis in Weber's work - small wonder, since Fayol was seventeen years Weber's senior and spoke a different language. It is questionable whether Fayol ever did have the influence ascribed to him by later authors. His *magnum opus*, the *Administration Industrielle et Générale* was published when Fayol was in his mid-seventies, in 1916, and did not appear in English until 1949. Perhaps most surprisingly, for a work of such little merit, Burns and Stalker accept that Fayol's ideas still influenced organisational analysis some eighty years after he committed them to paper.

By the standards of scientific method, therefore, - and sociology aspires to be a social science - few if any of the influential studies of the pioneers of Cellular Manufacturing can be accepted as valid sociological research. Scientific investigation is passive - the process of measurement must not influence the behaviour of the system itself. Thus those researchers who sought to justify the social benefits of Group Technology - Edwards, Fazakerley, Burbidge and their co-workers - were driven by a desire to improve the quality of the working environment. They had committed the cardinal sin of sociology - they had personal social objectives - thereby corrupting the objectivity of their studies. Exactly the same charges could be - and indeed were - (justifiably) placed regarding the work of Elton Mayo and his researchers. Brown (1954) remarked:

> *His theses ... may be confidently accepted as valid, and their validity is not affected by the criticisms as to method, bias, and the lack of sociological background ...*

The failure of modern sociologists to acknowledge that the founders of their discipline were practice-driven empiricists is, at best, disingenuous and, at worst, downright dishonest. It is justifiable to report early studies whilst remarking on subsequent criticism of their methodology; it is inexcusable to exclude them from future commentary on this basis. Are sociological investigations to be reported on the basis of the purity of the investigational protocol or on the basis of their potential to contribute to change? - *value or validity?*

Even where sociologists make all reasonable attempts to ensure the scientific validity of their work, it is certain to contain innate bias. As Brown (1954) suggested, the validity of industrially based research is contextual. In particular, Brown's typical industrialist is motivated by the need to .... *make a profit and make goods.* Thus the gathering of industrial data must be justified either in reference to these aims or by appeal to the altruism of the industrialist. The result is either a group of co-operating partners with (dishonestly gained) inappropriate expectations or a biased sample containing those industrialists with altruistic motives. Thus, like all disciplines, Napoleon's principle (the pig - not the emperor) applies:

All sociological research is biased - but some is more biased than others.

It should not be inferred that modern sociological research should be disregarded - nothing could be further from the truth. The work of Penn et al. (1994) contains a wealth of information which those who are entrusted with technological change neglect at their peril.

Hollier himself indicates some of the reasons for the problems in production research; he remarks: *Some of the firms visited were so lacking in production information and planned control that it would have been a waste of effort to spend time setting up a complete data collection system.* Hollier's study itself covered just two companies, a machine-tool company and a general engineering company manufacturing for both external customers and internal requirements. The latter was chosen on the basis that it was *deemed desirable* to choose a company outside the automotive market *due to its dominating influence.*

Whilst the inadequacy of management controls is often recognised when they are abandoned, the purpose of the changes is often then forgotten. A weakness of functional layout recognised by Gallagher was the difficulties of devising a representative costing structure. As Johnson and Kaplan (1987) have described, the deficiencies of the cost systems were well known when they were devised in the 1920s; indeed, the most common systems were devised when earlier more accurate methods became prohibitively expensive to maintain. The designers of the early cellular manufacturing system described by Flanders (1924) had explicitly rejected these accepted methods of cost accounting in the design of their system.

Consider the progress of a typical batch of components through the functionally organised factory. Perhaps a quality problem arises at a given stage: a proportion of the components are dimensionally out of tolerance:

It is unlikely that the individual operative is aware of the consequences of the error for this particular component; often it would take a skilled manufacturing engineer considerable effort to resolve such a question. Often engineering components are over-designed, so that in the vast majority of cases small dimensional errors never compromise the functional performance of the product.

If the defect is reported, the operative's remuneration may be compromised through retention of bonuses or reductions in piece-rate allowances. The operative's status may be threatened if components are found to be out of specification repeatedly. In short, there is often every incentive for the operative to conceal the fault.

Assuming the defect is not identified or - perhaps more often - if its occurrence is suppressed, then there is every likelihood that it will take days, weeks or months before it is discovered. From the nature of the defect, it is likely that the shop in which it occurred will be readily deduced but it may take considerably more effort to identify the individual machinist. Because the planned time of delivery to the customer is looming - or already past - management attention is usually more likely to be focused on restitution than on retribution. Typically it is only when repeated instances of poor workmanship are traceable to a machine shop that action is taken to resolve quality problems.

In passing through the factory each batch will accrue a number of defective components. Usually these are obvious and the components discarded; occasionally components with multiple defects are seen. The traditional approach to the loss of components from a batch is not to spend considerable amounts of management effort attempting to resolve the manufacturing problems but to build in scrap allowances into the order quantity. If the allowances are too generous then stocks of uncommitted components build up in the finished-goods stores; if they are too parsimonious then quantities of kits of components with shortages are likely to build up in the assembly stages of the manufacturing system. Either way, and probably both ways, large stocks of commercially useless components are likely to accrue.

Kits of parts with shortages will probably correspond to a customer expectation - unless this has been anticipated by building in further scrap allowances. Even in the most incompetent of manufacturing organisations customer delivery complaints are regarded as important even where their requirements cannot or should not be satisfied. (An age-old principle of production control - totally discredited and discreditable - is: *Serve the customer who shouts the loudest*). The most common response to such shortages is the designation of small priority batches - much less than an economic batch quantity - driven through production by expediters (the technical term for progress chasers) using a mixture of bribery, flattery and coercion.

What lessons can be learned from this case?

In the case described here, it has been assumed implicitly (and deliberately) that the failure to meet the tolerances for the component stemmed from a failure in manufacturing at the operative level. This is a typical and widespread assumption. An equally credible explanation, however, is that unrealistic expectations by a designer make the component impossible to produce to specification by the manufacturing technology available. Alternatively, the production machines may be old or poorly maintained, making them unable to perform to specification. So the symptoms of a quality problem may well appear far from their source. Where fault is assigned - and it often is not - it may be an innocent party who is blamed. As Deming had observed, organisations should seek to remove the need for mass inspection by building quality into the product - in this case by assigning priority to **design for manufacture**. Deming suggested that the cost of rework could account for as much as 40% of manufacturing costs. Perhaps more important is the diversion and dissipation of management effort into activities which add no value to the product and otherwise do nothing but generate dissatisfaction. (See, for example, Wille 1992.) Wille notes that wherever Deming went: *he found* *himself talking about management, which had lost sight of quality in the endless search for quantity and cost cutting.*

How would production controllers respond? Beyond the immediate impact of the defective product, the fact that an unknown proportion of a given batch fails at each stage of production leads either to an enormous effort to maintain data integrity or - probably more commonly - to a fatalistic acceptance that the eventual output from the manufacturing system is only quantifiable within a large margin of error. For safety of supply, excessive quantities of particularly vulnerable components will be scheduled into production.

Like most other functional groups, the sales department is likely to respond to the quality problem by using those powers under its own control. Even if the sales department recognises a problem of shortages before the production controller, it will, in general, be unable to distinguish between tardiness - the work is flowing too slowly through production, in competition with other batches, to satisfy demand - or rejection - sufficient components are scheduled but the rejection rate is eliminating too many components. To ensure continuity of supply, its ultimate decision will be to procure externally: for components of excessively demanding tolerances its suppliers will quote correspondingly higher prices; where there is a problem of manufacturing management, the prices are likely to be similar but delivery promises both more attractive and more likely to be honoured. Only then would the sales department be in a position to discriminate between these two possible failures in the management of the product. Unfortunately, once a secure supply is established, at an acceptable cost, the group is likely to consider that it has fulfilled its primary responsibility to the organisation. Very little benefit would be seen in alerting the organisation to a defect in its operating performance.

How then, could the substantial accrued craft experience - which - after all - was the whole rationale of establishing process-based production systems in the first place - be exploited? Taylor's approach to the organisation of manufacturing in the functional organisation was to generate a new class of management, the indirect specialist: the rate fixer, the inspector, etc. Each of these groups had direct access into each functional area but with a strictly constrained authority. Assuming the operative or the shop-floor supervisor had any residual initiative, it is likely that the approval of several indirect authorities would have to be obtained.

As Leonard and Rathmill (1977) observed, it is unreasonable to make comparisons between new Group Technology systems, which had had the benefit of detailed analysis from the most competent of engineers, and traditional functionally based systems, which had evolved rather than been designed. The proper comparison is between GT and **optimised** functional systems. Their prescription is the only true measure of competitive effectiveness: *effective management.*

The main emphasis here has been on inventory. This is important for a number of reasons: it represents a non-performing asset; it occupies a considerable amount of unproductive factory space; it disrupts material flow;... In any batch manufacturing system, simple strategies of inventory conversion should be considered:

> *Critical review of procurement policies;*
>
> *Elimination of unsaleable products in working inventories (scrap, obsolete, etc.);*
>
> *Completion of part-finished assemblies;*
>
> *Delivery of finished goods to customers.*

(from Brandon 1992).

Each of these approaches involves a different functional group (purchasing, finance, production and sales, respectively). Thus any effective programme of inventory conversion is necessarily multi-disciplinary.

The capacity for companies to underestimate excesses of inventory is occasionally portrayed as an exaggeration. However, van de Vliet (1990) recounts a case which is scarcely credible: a new managing director at a British forging company asked his staff to estimate their inventory. Their best *guess* was 500 tonnes; his own *estimate* was 10000 tonnes; the *stock take* revealed 30000 tonnes! The excess inventory generated £1.5m in the first ten days and £5m in three months.

As has been remarked before (Brandon 1992), addressing the last of these two problems reveals a great deal about the health of a company's manufacturing organisation.

Whatever the chosen structure of manufacturing systems in a factory, there are simple performance measures which can be applied generally to both existing manufacturing systems and candidate alternatives. These include: stock-turns per year, stock value to turnover ratio, etc. In the latter part of his career Burbidge concentrated the majority of his attention on these. Whilst retaining his faith in Group Technology, maintaining that process organisation results in *incredibly complex material flow systems* (Burbidge 1985), he recognised that production management systems must, in practice, be designed around a predominantly functional organisational structure (Burbidge 1988). His six-part recipe for achieving industrial competitiveness entailed:

- *Simple flow systems* - again explicitly warning against the complexities of process-based systems;

- *Total Quality Control* - As has been described above, the consequences of even modest levels of defective components can result in an unacceptable level of disruption and expense in maintaining the data integrity of the production control system in process-based systems. He contrasts the Western tolerance of substandard processes to the Japanese attitude where they would rather close down the process than accept defective components for integration into their products.

- *Just-in-Time production control* (JIT) - This, in itself, has major beneficial implications for the organisation of the business: stock is implicitly minimised; inter-operation storage is eliminated; obsolete products are not hidden within the inventory; the system tends to be responsive to customer choice; defective processes just cannot be tolerated.

- *Zero stock* - as has been remarked, stock constitutes a non-performing asset.

- *Delegation* - Burbidge highlights the absurdity of the viewpoint that clerks in offices can better judge how best to address decisions that only concern shop-floor activities than can the shop-floor workers themselves.

- *Use Management generalists.*

These measures are mutually reinforcing. JIT is intolerant of defective components. Once the quality problems are overcome, variability in the predictability of yield of batches is eliminated. Thus the deliberate production of excess stock through reject allowances is no longer justifiable. If all components are completed when expected then the clutter of kits of parts with shortages is avoided. As Skinner (1971) observed, however, all of these aspects of manufacturing management are inter-linked and cannot be approached in a piecemeal fashion.

Perhaps it is proper to allow John Burbidge to have the last word. In his last paper, published posthumously, Burbidge (1995) made a similar plea for the view of production management as a holistic applied science to be revived. He remarked that:

> *Forty years ago ... Production management was ..: the planning, direction and control of the manufacture and distribution of goods, in factories and their supply and distribution systems. Each company plans the whole of its own supply-manufacture-distribution system. Each of these three parts affects the efficiency of the others, and they cannot safely be treated in isolation.*

References

J A Brandon, 1992, Managing Change in Manufacturing Systems, Productivity Publishing, Olney, England.

104

J L Burbidge, 1985, A future for the engineering industry, First International Conference on Engineering Management: Theory and Applications, (Editors D J Leech et al.) University College, Swansea, 141-149.

J L Burbidge, 1988, IM before CIM, Twenty-seventh International Machine Tool Design and Research Conference, (Editor, B J Davies) UMIST/Macmillan Education, Basingstoke, England.

J L Burbidge, 1995(April), Back to production management, Manufacturing Engineer, 74(2), 66-71.

T Burns and G M Stalker, 1994, The Management of Innovation, Oxford University Press.

R E Flanders, 1924, Design, Manufacture, and Production Control of a Standard Machine, Transactions of the American Society of Mechanical Engineers, 46, 691-738.

C C Gallagher, April 1981 The history of batch production and functional factory layout, Chartered Mechanical Engineer, pp73-76.

R H Hollier, 1964, Two studies of work flow control, International journal of production Research, 3(4), 253-283.

H T Johnson and R S Kaplan, 1987, Relevance Lost: The Rise and Fall of Management Accounting, Harvard Business School Press.

R Leonard and K Rathmill, 1977 (January), The Group Technology myths, Management Today, 66-69.

R Gillespie, 1993, Manufacturing Knowledge: A history of the Hawthorne experiments, Cambridge University Press, Cambridge, England.

R Penn, 1994, Technical Change and Skilled Manual Work in Contemporary Rochdale, in Penn et al., 1994.

R Penn, M Rose and J Rubery 1994, Skill and Occupational Change, Oxford University Press.

R J Schonberger, 1990, Building a Chain of Customers: Linking Business Functions to Create the World Class Company, Hutchinson Business Books, London.

W Skinner, 1971 (January-February), The anachronistic factory, Harvard Business Review, 61-70.

A van de Vliet, 1990, Out of the furnace, Management Today, 50-55.

D T N Williamson, 1968 The pattern of batch manufacture and its influence on machine tool design, Proceedings of the Institution of Mechanical Engineers, 182, 870-895.

E Wille, 1992, Quality: Achieving Excellence, Century Business, London.

A CRISIS OF ORGANISATION

The evolution of the enterprise proceeds as an alternating sequence of evolution and revolution (Greiner 1972). Revolutionary stages are preceded by crises. The timing and severity of the crisis depend on a number of factors, mostly internal to the organisation. Because of their nature, manufacturing systems are immensely robust - they can tolerate an enormous amount of stress without yielding. Indeed much of manufacturing management effort is dissipated in crisis management. Under conditions of radical change, nobody can be sure of either their status or even their continuity of employment. Innovations in organisation are likely to require additional workloads and the expenditure of emotional energy. Thus there is an innate tendency to resist change.

A consensus prevailed throughout manufacturing on the superiority of process-based production organisation over product-based systems for batch manufacture until shortly after the second world war. As is common in organisational management, this consensus was due more to familiarity than to rational analysis.

As is by no means unusual, the focus of change was far from the primary centres of manufacturing industry - in the Soviet Union. Their crisis could no longer be averted. Their economy was ravaged; the core of their skills base - the adult male population - had been all but destroyed; the need for re-equipment of primary industries - not least agriculture and machine tools - was urgent and had the attention of a less than benign political administration. Although some work had been undertaken by A P Sokolovsky prior to the second world war, particularly in the machine-tool industry, credit for integrating this into a coherent manufacturing philosophy is usually attributed to S P

Mitrofanov (1966). The detail of the development of Group Technology in the USSR has been described in some detail by Grayson (1981).

The problems confronting the Soviet engineers may be advantageously viewed as a set of stimulus-response pairs:

Stimulus	Response
scarce materials	intolerance of inventory
scarce skills	multi-skilling
no capital available for investment in machines	optimum usage of existing plant

In contrast to the traditional management practices in the West, the Soviet engineers treated these issues as a coherent programme rather than as a set of unrelated problems.

The Soviet engineers provided a rigorous basis for their system designs. They recognised that Group Technology had been used to describe different concepts and regarded it as important to resolve difficulties in definition. Grayson (1983) quotes Burbidge (reporting on the First International Seminar on Group Technology in Turin, 1969) that: *The name is used by different people with different meanings.* Already, from Grayson's analysis, opportunities for misunderstanding of the basic concepts were observed. Even at this early stage, the Soviet engineers were emphasising that Group Technology was one of a range of strategic options for manufacturing and counselling against its adoption as a panacea.

The Soviet engineers distinguished between *group production* - applicable to primary manufacturing processes: forging, moulding, casting, etc. - and *group working* - relating to secondary processes such as metal cutting.

Grayson remarked that the role of GT in job enrichment had been the focus of considerable attention in the West but noted that, with only a single exception, he could find very little analysis of social effects in Group Technology. He used Fazakerley's checklist of sociological indicators (1974) to evaluate the Soviet approach to social analysis in Group Technology:

- The majority of the problem derives from the wider political and social environment in the USSR. The whole ethos of the Soviet system *was worker participation* - however specious was the reality. Thus it would be a brave engineer or social scientist who would even hold the concept up to critical evaluation.

- There was simply no evidence on *variety of tasks.*

- The issue of *meaningful pay incentives* similarly has to be considered in the wider political and social context. Local management simply did not have the discretion - tantamount to the political recklessness - to negotiate local pay agreements which suited the group methods of working.

- Once again, under centralised planning, management simply did not have the power to contemplate *redefining management roles.*

- There was some limited evidence that Group Technology had enhanced *operators' status.* This seemed to be due to increased independence of action rather than as a response to the improvements in technology.

- Grayson notes that there simply is no mention of *skill usage* in research where one could reasonably expect its analysis. He discusses *job flexibility, enlargement and flexibility,* remarking that they seem real but the references are largely implicit.

- On the issue of *training*, Grayson observes that this is one aspect where the Soviet and Western literature is in accord - it is virtually never mentioned in either! Similarly, although effective *communication* is widely regarded as essential for successful change management, its success rate had been low in both the USSR and the West.

Thus the Soviet pioneers of Group Technology portrayed, and probably saw, the design of GT systems as a technical organisational task rather than a social issue. It may well be that the Soviet engineers discussed such factors among themselves - from the implicit messages it seems extremely likely - but it would be a brave researcher indeed who would express ideas publicly which would tend to subvert the tenets of communism. As Burbidge had observed, there is no generally accepted measure of job satisfaction, even in the West, so the Soviet researchers would have been foolhardy to attempt to establish such indicators in a system where economic, technological, social and political systems were linked through the rigid framework of dialectical materialism.

It is evident from the historical record that Soviet engineers had brought Group Technology to a state of considerable sophistication. From Grayson's analysis, it appears that they had foreseen, and managed to avoid, many of the pitfalls which were to be experienced in Western Europe in the 1970s, as had Flanders (1924) in his pioneering paper in the 1920s.

REFERENCES

T J Grayson, 1981 (July), Group Technology in the USSR: conditions and prospects, Chartered Mechanical Engineer, 30.
G M Fazakerley, 1974, Group Technology: social benefits and social problems, The Production Engineer, 383-386.
R E Flanders, Design, Manufacture and Production Control of a Standard Machine, Transactions of the ASME, Volume 46, 1924, 691-738.
L E Greiner 1972 (July-August) Evolution and revolution as organizations grow, Harvard Business Review, 37-46.
S P Mitrofanov, 1966, Scientific Principles of Group Technology, British Library Lending Division Translation.

GROUP TECHNOLOGY: ORGANISATION, TECHNOLOGY AND MANAGEMENT

There have been many definitions of Group Technology. As has been remarked previously (Brandon 1992), *it has been presented variously as a philosophy, a strategy and/or a set of management techniques.* With a few rather eccentric exceptions, they conform to the philosophical aim defined by the author previously:

> *Group Technology seeks to obtain the ECONOMIES OF SCALE OF MASS PRODUCTION IN A BATCH-PRODUCTION ENVIRONMENT.*

> (Brandon 1992)

Mass production has a number of features which distinguish it from typical batch-production systems. The attractions for the pioneers of Group Technology were, however, rarely based on cost directly, but rather indirectly as a result of having more effective control over the manufacturing system.

Economies of scale are attained by eliminating - so far as is possible - non-productive costs. In batch manufacture these are dominated by the set-up costs and the inventory-holding costs. Recalling the formula for Economic Production Quantity,

$$Q_o = \sqrt{\frac{2SA}{H(1-D/P)}}$$

Where
Qo = *economic production quantity*
S = *Set-up cost*
A = *Annual usage rate*
H = *Annual unit holding cost*
D = *Daily usage rate*
P = *Daily production rate,*

it can be seen that these two cost elements have opposite effects on EPQ. High set-up costs have to be distributed through all components in a batch, thus making Q_0 high. High holding costs appear in the denominator of the formula, tending to reduce EPQ. That the formula is largely irrelevant in mass production can, however, be seen from the other component of the denominator: if the daily production rate and the daily usage rate are equal then the denominator will be zero and the effective EPQ will be infinite.

A number of manufacturing strategies can be constructed and evaluated on the basis of this formula:

- Attention can be focused on minimising the set-up time for each batch of components - reducing the distributed contribution of set-up costs (per batch) to unit costs (per component);

- Priority can be given to increasing the ratio of daily usage rate to daily production rate (permitting continuous steady flow through the system):

- The holding cost can be set at an arbitrarily punitive level (penalising inter-operation storage).

Much of the managerial rationale of Cellular Manufacturing Systems is that EPQ should be seen as a qualitative measure of the characteristics of a process rather than a quantitative managerial statistic. Some aspects of machine set-up are inevitable - even in fully automated systems, sensors have to be calibrated and tool offsets entered. The tasks for management are, consequently, the minimisation of their effects. There are two principal effects:

The first is the direct effect on the machine-operator: the machine cannot produce components; in many systems the operator is idle, or (infrequently) otherwise occupied, whilst a skilled toolsetter changes the machine set-up. This is quantified in the EPQ formula.

The second effect is often not associated with set-up, but it is an inevitable factor in the formation of the queues that bedevil batch manufacture. Even if both operator and machine are free when a particular batch of components arrive for processing, the batch cannot be processed unless the machine has beeen set for it. Thus queues can form even when machines and operators are idle. The more variable the products, the more likely this is to happen. Thus the formation of families of parts, with common set-ups, means that production runs on each machine can be much longer. Grouping machines to match the process routes of part families ensures that less set-up is required in the first place and also allows the use of jigs and fixtures specialised to the family. A (justified) criticism of Group Technology was the reduction of utilisation of the machine, but this can be exploited to allow the operator and setter (if a specialist setter is any longer required) to work together to arrange machine set-ups when the machine would otherwise be idle.

A principle which has received universal approval, but is rarely observed in practice, is that manufacturing management must be treated as a holistic problem. Burbidge (1995) uses the term *production management* rather more generally thando most authors. He defines it in terms of eight functional activities:

- *product design;*
- *production planning;*

- *production control;*

- *purchasing and the supply system;*

- *marketing, sales and the distribution system;*

- *finance, controls expenditure (sic), revenue, money flow and profit;*

- *personnel, employment, organisation and training;*

- *secretarial and data processing.*

To these specific functions, he adds *a general management function.*

Burbidge contends that traditionally the functional groupings have formed the basis for manufacturing organisation, but this is not necessary - he uses the word *mandatory.* Dependent on context, there can be significant advantages in forming employees into multi-disciplinary teams or *task forces* working on a single task or small range of activities. At the strategic level, this is currently described as **Concurrent Engineering** (Brandon 1995). A special case at a lower level of organisation is **Group Technology** (Burbidge 1995). Although the term is new, Concurrent Engineering is clearly described by Drucker - including the concept of *task forces* - in the mid 1950s (Drucker 1955). It has been suggested (Brandon 1995) that Concurrent Engineering is the natural state of organisation in the entrepreneurial organisation but this structure is difficult to sustain in the mature corporation. Thus both Concurrent Engineering and Group Technology - and other related concepts, such as the factory-within-a-factory - can be visualised as strategies to restore the values of the entrepreneurial enterprise in the mature organisation.

The attractive features of the small enterprise are:

- Multi-skilled operatives in small working groups;

- A small range of products;

- A limited installed base of (usually simple) production technology.

From / To	Design	production planning	production control	purchasing and supply	marketing	finance	personnel	secretarial
Design	X	Value analysis	quality control data (rejects, etc.)	material cost and availability data	New product specifications	Budgets and budgetary control	staff recruitment, training	Maintenance of design database
production planning	manufacturing technical requirements	X	production flow analysis (PFA)	make or buy decisions	Market priorities	Budgets and budgetary control	staff recruitment, training	Maintenance of product layout files
production control	bills of materials	process layouts	X	internal orders	market estimates	Budgets and budgetary control	staff recruitment, training	maintain schedules
purchasing and supply	make or buy requirements	schedules of components	capacity estimates, shortages and rejects	X	market estimates	Budgets and budgetary control	staff recruitment, training	stock control records
marketing	new product concepts	delivery estimation data	delivery commitments	identify competitive processes /products	X	Budgets and budgetary control	staff recruitment, training	customer and market reports
finance	material cost estimating	production cost estimating	shop loading data	cash-flow assessments	market estimates/sales data	X	staff recruitment, training	financial status information
personnel	training needs	training needs	training needs	training needs	training needs	training needs	X	maintain personnel records
secretarial	master drawing lists	Creation of product-layout files	capacity estimates, shortages and rejects	stock control records	personnel records	Budgets and budgetary control	staff recruitment, training	X

Typical communication processes in manufacturing systems

Contrast this with a typical large batch-manufacturing organisation with single-craft operators utilising a wide variety of machines - even within a single functional workshop - to manufacture an enormous range of products. Often some of these are produced to meet a steady demand, some are produced occasionally to special order and many are produced intermittently with no identifiable pattern of demand. (Skinner (1974) had illustrated the problems with this type of product mix.) Small wonder that many batch manufacturers seem to thrive only in conditions as close to chaos as makes no difference. The working conditions are characterised by clutter, congestion and a constant atmosphere of urgency - though rarely eliciting an appropriate response - from shop-floor supervisors.

Group Technology addresses these issues as a single coherent problem:

- Components are aggregated into families with similar production requirements;
- Small groups of machines (either cells, without sequential material handling, or flow-lines, where handling systems are integrated to exploit sequential material flow) are matched to the component families;
- Groups of operatives are assigned to cells or flow-lines.

One of the best overviews of Group Technology is provided by Hyer and Wemmerlöv (1984) in the Harvard Business Review. Subsequent papers by Wemmerlöv and Hyer (1986, 1987) are also cogent and relevant. That one of the best papers was written for a general audience is perhaps best explained by the observation by Edwards and Fazakerley (1973) that: *Too often the minor importance of the techniques has been over-emphasized at the expense of the people they serve.*

In many respects the problems of relevance are becoming more acute with ever more sophisticated techniques, often of doubtful advantage over their predecessors, being applied either to representative standard sets of historical records or on simulated data. The accessibility and industrial relevance of these academic studies are becoming increasingly difficult to justify with each dissertation produced. The literature is enormous; a comprehensive bibliography published in 1983 lists 451 papers, including two other bibliographies, three surveys, two reviews and nine books (Waghodekar and Sahu 1983).

Even then, the authors: *do not claim the completeness of the bibliography, but believe that it will be found useful to practitioners as well as researchers.* Waghodekar and Sahu categorise the research according to four aspects:

- Formation of cells with minimal inter-cell flows;
- Determination of number of cells and their sizes;
- Workload balancing and machine utilisation;
- Effects on costing, wage payment methods and organisational behaviour.

Hyer and Wemmerlöv (1984) contend that the organisational advantages of Group Technology have three primary aspects:

- Performing similar activities together;
- Standardising closely related activities;
- Efficient storage and retrieval of information.

Put in these terms, Group Technology seems such an obvious strategic development in the regeneration of the batch-based manufacturing enterprise that its adoption seems natural. As Wemmerlöv and Hyer (1987) observe, Group Technology can be ... *one critical element in the rejuvenation of outdated and unproductive plant.*

Thus, at first sight, the rationale for Group Technology is principally a technical issue, based on product type, product mix, market conditions, etc. There is a large body of evidence that this is too simplistic an approach and that attitudinal factors can make or break a Group Technology system, or more generally other types of Cellular Manufacturing System or wider organisational strategies such as Concurrent Engineering. Wemmerlöv and Hyer (1987) remark:

... applicability for a particular firm is not merely a technical issue .... but also hinges on the organisation's readiness for Cellular Manufacturing and the actions taken by the firm during system implementation.

References

J A Brandon, 1995, Concurrent engineering and manufacturing infrastructure, Fifth International Conference on Flexible Automation and Integrated Manufacturing, Stuttgart (Editors, R D Schraft et al.), Begell House, New York, 1124-1133.

J L Burbidge, 1995(April), Back to production management, Manufacturing Engineer, 74(2), 66-71.

P F Drucker, 1955, The Practice of Management, Heinemann Professional Publishing (1989 reprint), Oxford.

G A B Edwards and G M Fazakerley, 1973, The cell system of production embraces group technology and also concerns management, technical and social change, Proceedings of the 14th Machine Tool Design and Research Conference (Editors, F Koenigsberger and S Tobias), Manchester, 197-206.

N L Hyer and U Wemmerlöv, 1984 (July-August), Group technology and productivity, Harvard Business Review, 140-149.

W Skinner 1974 (May-June), The focused factory, Harvard Business Review, 113-121; also in V Bignell et al. (Editors), 1985, Manufacturing Systems: Context, Applications and Techniques, Open University /Blackwell, Oxford.

P H Waghodekar and S Sahu, 1983, Group Technology: A Research Bibliography, OPSEARCH 20(4), 225-249.

U Wemmerlöv and N L Hyer, 1986, Procedures for the Part Family/Machine Group Identification Problem in Cellular Manufacturing, Journal of operations Management, 6(2), 125-147.

U Wemmerlöv and N L Hyer, 1987, Research issues in cellular manufacturing, International Journal of Production Research, 25(3), 413-431.

D T N Williamson, 1968, The pattern of batch manufacture and its influence on machine tool design, Proceedings of the Institution of Mechanical Engineers, 182, 870-895.

FORMATION OF PART FAMILIES: RIGHTS AND WRONGS

The formation of part families is generally accepted as the first stage in Group Technology. If this stage is bungled then the chances of recovery are slight. Various options are available, and the potential success of these is fundamentally based on the self-awareness of the business. Managers responsible for strategic development need to answer frankly the question: **What is the basis of our business?**

Perhaps the most unusual answer was that of the Molins company, of which Theo Williamson was responsible for production research. The solution to their family formation problem - as might be expected - was unique (Williamson 1968). As with many of the more long-lasting of Cellular Manufacturing Systems, the Molins system was based on a classification originating in the design function. Although the classification system devised by Molins is unlikely to be suitable for the majority of companies, the description of the reasoning behind the design decisions provided by Williamson is applicable to any company contemplating the introduction of a classification system.

Design-based classification systems already existed, most notably the Brisch system (advocated by Joseph Gombinsky 1969 - see also Baer 1985), the Miclass system (originating at TNO in the Netherlands, Vos 1979) and - perhaps the best known of all - the Opitz system, developed at the Technical University of Aachen (Opitz 1970). An excellent overview of these classification systems is given by Gallagher and Knight (1986).

As Vos (1979) remarked, without a design-based classification system a company is unable, in general, to recall whether a part to fulfil a given function has been designed before. As will be seen, Williamson (1968) did not see this as an unqualified benefit. Thus the first function of a classification system is in design retrieval. The majority of classification systems generate a shape code which often proves sufficient to compare a new part specification to existing parts. Part codes are usually sufficiently detailed to include planar and rotational symmetries, internal and external cutting, threads, aspect ratios and assembly features such as keyways.

Williamson (1968) took the view that the emphasis on design retrieval itself may lead a company into damaging decisions. He suggested that the opportunity for a designer to be given access to such a design database provides a temptation -even if such a practice is not actively encouraged - to use existing components - perhaps inappropriately - rather than design products optimised to their specification, and   ... *is a complete misconception of the object of design.* He contends that there is a tendency to *stultify* design, transforming it from a creative activity into a routine process of assembling existing parts. Thus the uncritical use of design-retrieval systems *puts a premium on the suppression of novelty, which is clearly a disastrous thing to do ...* Compromises are made which - far from the objective of reducing costs - tend to increase both design and manufacturing costs. They also tend to perpetuate and reinforce inefficient and outdated manufacturing methods.

Williamson's (1968) commentary is rather disingenuous. It is usual for advocacy of classification systems to be accompanied by a strong recommendation that design retrieval should only be used in combination with value analysis. (The books by Miles (1961) and Gage (1967) are still regarded as the definitive texts on value analysis.) In value analysis a sequence of simplistic questions (Gage uses twelve) is asked about the product:

- What function(s) does the component/product fulfil?
- How much does it cost?
- How complex is it?
- What is the demand: historical, current, projected?

- How else could the purpose be achieved?

- What would be the cost of other options?

- Can the product be enhanced by increasing/reducing its range of functions?

- How can the improvements be implemented?

Lockyer (1974) emphasises the necessity for value analysis to be carried out by a team or task force. In particular, he recommends the co-option of *intelligent laymen* who *have no special case to plead or cause to defend.*

There is little doubt, from the anecdotal evidence, that design-retrieval systems have been misused in exactly the manner Williamson (1968) described. However, as with many system failures, the fault is not in the design of the system but rather in its utilisation. A general shape-coding system is ideal in companies with a wide variety of component shapes in relatively balanced quantities. It is invaluable in design retrieval and value analysis; it enables first-pass process layouts to be prepared; it simplifies cost estimating. It is particularly appropriate for sub-contract batch manufacturing where the shape code will determine the capability of the manufacturing system to produce the component, particularly where sub-codes indicate quality standards, and will be of some assistance in cost estimating and capacity planning. Companies can provide preliminary cost and delivery estimates based solely on the code, machine capability files and current schedules.

Design retrieval is an activity which takes place within a single function. There is, however, a different inter-functional use for a shape-classification system, that of conveying component geometry from design into process planning. If the shape code indicates any external cylindrical features then it can be inferred that a turning or cylindrical grinding operation is required. (The implicit distinction between these two processes is transmitted in some classification systems using a subsidiary code to define surface finish.)

Williamson (1968) expressed doubts whether classification by geometry is the best method. In assessing the relevance of general classification systems to Molins, Williamson (1968) praised their *considerable ingenuity* but suggested that they were capable of *hair-splitting pedantry.* He suggested that, in a given organisation, no more than twenty or thirty component classes would be needed, ... *in which case the allocation of an individual component to a group becomes obvious ....*

Surprisingly, Williamson (1968) compares shape classification unfavourably to the most common of traditional alternative design-office systems - Williamson says it *has more to recommend it* - which shape classifications had replaced in many manufacturing organisations. In many companies this entails the allocation of part numbers on a simple sequential basis. When a designer is requested to produce a new component, there is no inbuilt mechanism for retrieving earlier designs which might fulfil the defined purpose. Only the most conscientious of designers will search the drawing files for a similar - perhaps identical - component known to exist. Where the designer does investigate availability, it is likely to be on the basis of memory and/or personal records. Even in the case of simple items - nuts, bolts, washers, etc. - the same component may have several different code numbers. Some assemblies may not be completed because of perceived shortages of components under one part number when an identical component is stored under a different code.

Williamson's (1968) approach was a classification system based on end use. He observed that a shape classification would have difficulty in distinguishing between ... *a barge-pole and a retaining pin* ... but that their manufacturing processes would be completely different. If components are classified according to their eventual application, however, there are implicit conditions on their manufacturing process layout. For example, a component described as a **shaft** is used to transmit rotational power and is necessarily cylindrical. Thus, as described previously, a turning operation is almost inevitable - most probably linked to cylindrical grinding for the bearing surfaces. The existence of other features - for example a keyway - is also probable. Also implicit in the description of a wide variety of products would be the materials, heat-treatments, surface finishes, etc.

Williamson's (1968) criticisms of the ineffectiveness of general classification systems are both selective and rather exaggerated. There are many classification systems - Burbidge (1979) lists 46 - each with differing strengths and weaknesses, and some contain the features which Williamson claims negate their effectiveness.

As has been mentioned, Molins was an untypical manufacturing enterprise, dominant in a niche market. Molins specialised in the production of tobacco-processing machinery. Such machines are characterised by repetitive operations at high speed and low load. They were able to classify their components into twenty-four categories, of which eleven were manufactured in *basic mechanical engineering cells,* three were specific to Molins machine tools, two were special to their tobacco machinery and eight were based around other miscellaneous components including finished bought-out assemblies, cable work, circuit boards, transducers, etc.

Williamson (1968) made claims for the advantages of his type of functional (in the sense of the function of the product rather than an organisational concept) classification system:

- The part groupings are natural and indicate their end use;
- The parts in a particular group are likely to share materials, processes and finishes;
- The performance characteristics of parts in the same group - fatigue, wear, etc. - are likely to be similar, requiring similar skills;
- In-house know-how - always difficult to define, is more easily understood and recognised; it is likely that it will be enhanced;
- Group pride in an identifiable product is probable;
- Manufacturing defects can be resolved at the point of occurrence through informal procedures rather than the formal processes of a functional organisation;
- Communication is enhanced. Williamson made it clear that, in his view, it was worthwhile to sacrifice other measures of effectiveness - such as machine utilisation -to gain these improvements in communication.

The Molins system was radically new in other respects. Specifically, Small (1983) identifies it as one of two contenders for the description of the world's first **Flexible Manufacturing System.** From his later writings, it is evident that Williamson (1974) appreciated this significance, but it seems clear that he considered his organisational innovations to be more important than his technological contributions. Small's contention will be discussed later when the characteristics of Flexible Manufacturing Systems are considered.

The use of a general classification system - whether based on shape, function or other product features - reinforces the viewpoint that Group Technology systems, and other similar methodologies, were special cases of Concurrent Engineering.

These two types of classification system implicitly take a holistic view of the manufacturing system in that different functions can use the information contained in the code as a basis for communication. The choice between these two approaches - and indeed a number of other options - relies on the management of the organisation making a frank appraisal of the nature of their business.

The need to involve a number of different functions of the organisation in cell formation was reduced - if not eliminated - by an innovation due to Burbidge (1989). As has been remarked, Burbidge regarded the problems of organisational effectiveness as being the first priority of the manufacturing enterprise. If the control systems are defective, then no amount of managerial intervention will avoid inefficiencies and frustrations. In short, prevention is better than cure. In terms of potential disruption and risk to the organisation, it is difficult to fault Burbidge's methodology, which was based on cell formation within a single function. It should also be recognised that the ultimate reward of cellular manufacturing is a culture change throughout the organisation. Thus Burbidge's ideas tended to narrow the focus of Group Technology - minimising the risk but lowering the potential reward.

Hussain and Leonard (1976) described a system, implemented in a turbine manufacturing plant, which was a combination of a design-based classification system - the Czech VUOSO system, which Gallagher and Knight (1986) suggest is particularly well suited to companies with a large proportion of rotational components - and data on the workpiece statistics. Gallagher and Knight suggest that this is a very attractive approach for companies with established and reliable production records but would be unsuitable for the design of new Group Technology systems.

Thus the type of part-family formation system, and implicitly cell formation methodology, may be a strategic decision for the whole organisation, involving all the business functions: design, production engineering, production control, procurement, marketing, etc., or may be restricted to a single function. Some businesses may have hybrid strategies according to their functional perceptions, for example product-design codes which span the whole organisation, across a number of sites, whilst allowing local autonomy to production engineers to undertake jig and tool design to gain maximum benefit from local employment agreements.

As Williamson (1968) explained, general shape classification coding systems are applicable in companies with a very broad and balanced range of parts. Such organisations are relatively unusual in manufacturing industry. More commonly, large parts of a general code, such as the Opitz system, are quite redundant. The discriminant between two similar components may reside in a very restricted portion of the code, which is insufficiently detailed to provide the information for analysing the production routes for cell formation. In a manufacturer of electrical switches, for example, a very small range of shapes are produced in a restricted set of materials: thermosetting plastics, copper, brass, etc. Components in the same material are likely to have similar functions, and hence similar shapes and common production routes.

Thus the choice of part-family formation system is large. It depends, to a large extent, on the organisation's strategic and operational self-assessment. It depends on perceptions of the past, present and future of the product range of the company. To this end, it must be linked to standard methods of strategic planning that management generalists use in other contexts.

References

A Baer, 1985 (November), With Group Technology, No One Reinvents the Wheel, Mechanical Engineering, 60-69.

J L Burbidge, 1979, Group Technology in the Engineering Industry, Mechanical Engineering Publications, London.

J L Burbidge, 1989, Production Flow Analysis, Oxford University Press.

W L Gage, 1967, Value Analysis, McGraw-Hill, London.

C C Gallagher and W A Knight, 1986, Group Technology production methods in manufacture, Ellis Horwood, Chichester, England.

J Gombinski, 1969, Fundamental Aspects of Component Classification, Annals of the CIRP, 17, 367-375.

M Hussain and R Leonard, 1976, The design of standard cells for Group Technology by use of machine tool and workpiece statistics, Proceedings of the Sixteenth Machine Tool Design and Research Conference, UMIST, Manchester, 87-98.

K G Lockyer, 1974, Factory and Production Management, Third Edition, Pitman, London.

L D Miles, 1961, Techniques of Value Analysis and Engineering, McGraw-Hill, New York.

H Opitz, 1970, A Classification to Describe Workpieces, Pergamon, Oxford.

W J Vos, Group Technology, 1979, What can it do for you? International Conference on Production Research, 49-53

B W Small, 1983, Wealth Generation - Our Essential Task, Proceedings of the Institution of Mechanical Engineers, 197B,131-141.

D T N Williamson, 1968, The pattern of batch manufacture and its influence on machine tool design, Proceedings of the Institution of Mechanical Engineers, 182, 870-895.

D T N Williamson, The Anachronistic Factory, Proceedings of the Royal Society, A331, 1972, 139-160.

CELL FORMATION USING PRODUCTION FLOW ANALYSIS

Although Burbidge published his his consolidated account of **Production Flow Analysis** only in 1989, it originates from a much earlier phase of activity in Europe - Gallagher and Knight (1986) give Burbidge (1975) as the authoritative reference. Much of the credit for the basic analysis is due to El-Essawy (1971) - and is credited so by Burbidge himself (1979).

Burbidge (1979) justifies his preference for using Production Flow Analysis for group formation, in contrast to classification and coding systems, remarking that the design-oriented methodologies are ... *efficient for variety reduction and design retrieval, for which they were originally designed, but are not satisfactory as a way of forming groups.*

The essential strength of Production Flow Analysis (PFA) is that cell formation can be accomplished within a single function; this is also its principal weakness. The production scheduling records contain information as to the sequence of machines visited by each component. There is a high probability that components with the same, or closely related, production routes will be exactly those components with similar functions or similar shapes which would be identified through a design-based classification system. Just as importantly, the production records contain information of the historical volume of each product. Thus the justification of PFA is based on Burbidge's (1975) contention that .... *families of components and groups of machines exist naturally.* Thus the primary task for the production engineer is the efficient and effective identification of these natural affinities.

Production Flow Analysis has three stages:

> *Factory flow analysis*: this segregates the total product range into categories - families-of-families - with primary production affinities, typically at the scale of a product-based department of the factory - leading to what would now be described as **factories-within-a-factory**;
>
> *Group analysis*: forms the families of products and groups of machines within the departments - **cell or flowline formation;**
>
> *Line analysis*: depending on the mix of volume and variety of the members of the family, forms the group of machines into the optimum configuration.

The mechanisms of formation of families and groups are extremely diverse, ranging from classical statistical techniques, such as cluster analysis, to their modern successors, neural nets, genetic algorithms, etc. Numerous *advances* in technical capability are announced each year, demonstrating - if nothing else - the health and vigour of the thesis industry. Often these techniques are only marginal advances over existing methods, and their superiority is demonstrated on *typical data sets*. How representative these data are is always open to question, since they are usually either synthesised or are real data from companies who have reasoned that they are so out-of-date that their commercial significance is no longer of importance. Reference to two or three recent issues of the *International Journal of Production Research* or *Annals of the CIRP* should provide sufficient appreciation of recent research.

In his own analysis, Burbidge (1979) integrates discussion of the three phases of PFA with commentary on how the techniques fit into the framework. The primary data for PFA comprise only three records:

- *an accurate plant list;*
- *a route card for each component;*
- *a used on record, generally in the form of a parts list for each component.*

Burbidge (1979) remarks that the accuracy of these records, particulary the first, cannot be assumed in many companies.

There is considerable merit in the argument that the more simple a method the more successful it is likely to be in industrial implementation. Perhaps the crudest method of all for line analysis is similar to that used by Parnaby et al. (1987), who define three categories of products: runners, repeaters and strangers.

Category of product	Description and treatment
Runners	Volume allows flowline methods of production layout; usually expected to have continuing demand; repetitive manufacturing methods; consider automation of materials handling for heavy/awkward components
Repeaters	Steady demand but insufficient to justify flowline layout; may have expectation of limited future demand (end of lifecycle or market uncertainty)
Strangers	Occasionally ordered; no clear distinction between process and product treatment in production control

References

J A Brandon, 1995, Concurrent engineering and manufacturing infrastructure, Fifth International Conference on Flexible Automation and Integrated Manufacturing, Stuttgart (Editors, R D Schraft et al.), Begell House, New York, 1124-1133.

J L Burbidge, 1975, The Introduction of Group Technology, Heinemann, London.

J L Burbidge, 1979, Group Technology in the Engineering Industry, Mechanical Engineering Publications, London.

J L Burbidge, 1989, Production Flow Analysis, Oxford University Press.

128

I F K El-Essawy, 1971, The development of component flow analysis in production systems design for multi-product companies, PhD thesis, University of Manchester Institute of Science and Technology.

C C Gallagher and W A Knight, 1986, Group Technology production methods in manufacture, Ellis Horwood, Chichester, England.

J Parnaby, P Johnson and B Herbison, 1987, Development of the JIT-MRP factory control system, Second International Conference on Computer-Aided Production Engineering, Edinburgh, Mechanical Engineering Publications, Bury St Edmunds, 17-22.

GROUP TECHNOLOGY IN THE CORPORATE CONTEXT

Two radically different approaches to Cellular Manufacturing in the area of Group Technology have been illustrated. To Williamson (1968,1974), all of the functional specialists must be involved in the design and implementation of Cellular Manufacturing. Group Technology can, and should, be the hub of a **task force** designed to improve the competitiveness of the business by making it more responsive to markets, technology and developments in management theory.

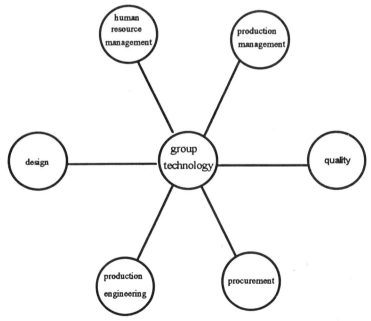

Group Technology in a concurrent environment

Although in his later works Burbidge (1995) emphasised the holistic nature of competitive manufacturing, the essence of Production Flow Analysis was that cell formation could - and probably should - be achieved as a technical and mechanistic activity within a single specialist functional group.

Burbidge (1979) specifically qualified the role of Group Technology in his reports on the humanisation of work, restricting it to: *the Production Engineering concept of Group Technology.*

Viewed as a specialised form of Concurrent Engineering, Group Technology can be visualised as a central focus of the organisation, involving all of the functional groups specified by Burbidge (1995). It is not surprising, however, that many companies saw Production Flow Analysis as the low-risk approach to Cellular Manufacturing. As with Scientific Management some sixty years earlier, where the rewards of the piece-rate system were seen as significantly more tangible than Taylor's other ideas, managers saw the majority of the benefit as being derived from a single aspect of Group Technology. Cells **could** be formed by a technique restricted to a single functional area; therefore they **should** be. The most visible aspect of cell formation became the dominant one.

There is merit in the proposition that general management should regularly assess the efficacy of the communication between those functional groups who are naturally involved with Group Technology - as they should review all relationships between specialist groups in the organisation.

Two primary problems are apparent when the interaction between technologists and general managers is examined (Brandon 1995):

- *There may be a mismatch of technological knowledge, experience and expertise which leads to different expectations of the eventual overall benefits of the technology;*

FUNCTION	ROLE WITHIN A CONCURRENT GROUP TECHNOLOGY SYSTEM
DESIGN	Product rationalisation value engineering classification and coding design retrieval
HUMAN RESOURCE MANAGEMENT	changes in supervisory structure elimination of craft demarcations reward systems which value quality and productivity training and re-training
PRODUCTION MANAGEMENT	production flow analysis cell formation managing supervisory structure
QUALITY	simplification of quality procedures empowerment of production operatives
PROCUREMENT	make-or-buy as strategic rather than operational decision internal customer philosophy
PRODUCTION ENGINEERING	customisation of machines/jigs / fixtures standardised set-up

Group Technology as an example of Concurrent Engineering

- *As with all problems with development and implementation of new technology, it is extremely difficult to match resource-allocation programmes to as yet unknown technical requirements.*

Where Group Technology was treated as a holistic philosophy it became a central focus of the objectives of the organisation (Brandon 1993, 1995). Each functional group had different local objectives and contributed different specialist skills, but each recognised that there was mutual benefit to be derived from cooperation, with a consequential overall benefit to the enterprise. This is, however, a high-risk strategy with uncertain rewards. Where a more conservative approach is available, apparently with similar benefits, it is natural for management to choose the safer course.

In a number of companies, Production Flow Analysis was seen as a cell-formation strategy which appeared to give all of the benefits of wider schemes of Group Technology - and in companies with certain characteristics this was certainly true - but without the necessary disruption to the structure of the organisation. As described previously (Brandon 1993, 1995) ... *cell formation became seen as the whole objective of Group Technology rather than just part of a wider process of strategic change.*

The consequence of this perception was that contributions of specialist groups outside the production-management disciplines tended to be underestimated and, ultimately, implicitly belittled. Where there is an erosion of esteem, commitment is liable to suffer. Even where loss of morale is not a problem, there is a tendency for specialists outside the principal function to feel that their interests are not being served. In many companies the issue of cellular manufacturing became isolated within the production-management function. As with Scientific Management sixty years earlier - where the piece-rate system was installed in isolation - the senior management saw merit in implementing only the part of Group Technology where immediate and appreciable benefits could be identified.

In this way, what has been described (Brandon 1993,1995) as *functional collapse* tended to occur. In some companies, functional groups outside Production Management had agreed to cooperate with the Cellular Manufacturing programme; their efforts had gone unrewarded in terms of either managerial esteem or the promised simplification of communications between themselves and other functional groups. In some cases their tasks became more arduous because of more demanding expectations from a significantly streamlined manufacturing system.

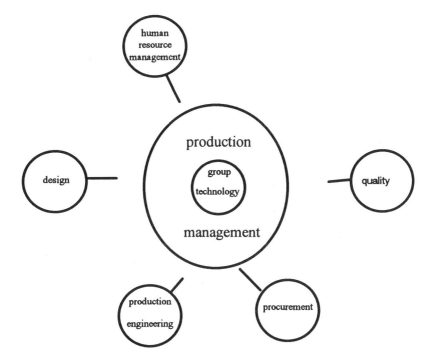

Functional collapse of Group Technology

In the present work the majority of the analysis has been devoted to a manufacturing systems paradigm - Group Technology - that has already been in existence for over fifty years. This has been justified:

> *Group Technology is a mature manufacturing systems philosophy which has a number of significant features in common with more general programmes of Concurrent Engineering. Whereas Concurrent Engineering has a present and a future, Group Technology also has a well documented past.*
>
> (Brandon 1995)

Thus the successes and failures of Group Technology are likely to be mirrored in other methodologies with the same type of organisational scope, whether these be more general systems of Cellular Manufacturing or related problems such as Concurrent Engineering. The lessons which can be learned from experience of Group Technology are:

- *The performance of separate sub-systems may not be completely transferable to integrated systems. This may be due to incompatibilities between the requirements or perspectives of different functional groups or to redundancies, i.e. common capabilities in different systems.*

- *That focusing on a single key issue may cause functional specialists who have no interest in that problem to become marginalised and reluctant to participate when an essential contribution is due.*

- *That no one functional group should be allowed to dominate the project and implicitly assume ownership of the idea.*

- *That cultural resistance to product-based organisational strategies requires that such programmes must be explicitly supported in statements of corporate strategy and that this commitment must be constantly reinforced - by deeds as well as words.*

- *That the timescales for technological change are almost always underestimated.*

- *That the effort require to introduce new technology is similarly estimated too optimistically.*

(Brandon 1995).

References

J A Brandon, 1993, On the vulnerability of interdisciplinary programmes of strategic change to functional interests: a case study, Journal of Strategic Change, 2(3), 151-156.

J A Brandon, 1995, Concurrent engineering and manufacturing infrastructure, Fifth International Conference on Flexible Automation and Intelligent Manufacturing, Stuttgart (Editors, R D Schraft et al.), Begell House, New York, 1124-1133.

J L Burbidge, 1979, A study of the effects of group production methods on the humanisation of work, Final report: International Centre for Advanced Technical and Vocational Training, Turin.

J L Burbidge, 1995(April), Back to production management, Manufacturing Engineer, 74(2), 66-71.

D T N Williamson, 1968, The pattern of batch manufacture and its influence on machine tool design, Proceedings of the Institution of Mechanical Engineers, 182, 870-895.

D T N Williamson, 1972, The anachronistic factory, Proceedings of the Royal Society, A331, 139-160.

UNCERTAINTY AND RESPONSIVENESS: FLEXIBLE MANUFACTURING SYSTEMS

As has been described, Group Technology seeks to exploit the management strategies of mass production. The manufacturing system is re-configured to achieve, so far as is possible, flow-line methods of production. Because of expectations about the future demand stability, it is possible to specialise the layout of production technology around the process routes of a small range of products.

Parnaby's simple classification of products into *runners, repeaters and strangers* places Flexible Manufacturing Systems (FMS) in context. The central objective of FMS has been articulated by a number of authors as the ***economic batch size of one.*** For this, set-up **at the machine** is eliminated completely by using flexible machines. This certainly does not mean that no preparatory work will be undertaken. Typically, FMS installations comprise an assembly of programmable machines (usually under numerical control) and handling equipment (usually robots). Components are commonly set manually onto standard pallets (Tempelmeier 1992). Process activities such as tool-path planning and materials handling are anticipated in design through CAD-CAM software. Thus these costs can be attributed directly to the product rather than assigned to manufacturing when the components are produced. Activities such as tool setting and sensor calibration must be costed but may now be allocated as direct costs of the machine rather than to a batch of components.

It is not the purpose of the current work to expound the technical details of the design or operation of Flexible Manufacturing Systems. In many respects it is surprising how close recent descriptions of Flexible Manufacturing Systems (see, for example, Tempelmeier 1992) are to **System 24**, designed by Williamson (1968) in the 1960s. As observed by

138

Small (1983), Williamson could reasonably claim the world's first Flexible Manufacturing System.

Browne et al. (1985) define eight dimensions of flexibility, defined hierarchically:

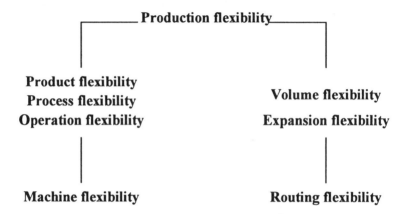

Types of flexibility and their relationships
(adapted from Browne et al. 1985).

Depending on the dimensions of flexibility of a particular application, Browne et al. (1985) define four types of Flexible Manufacturing System:

- *Type I FMS: Flexible Machining Cell;*
- *Type II FMS: Flexible Machining System;*
- *Type III FMS: Flexible Transfer Line;*
- *Type IV FMS: Flexible Transfer Multi-Line.*

Each of these types of system has varying degrees of the basic flexibility type. The same basic categories of cell/flowline were evident in the commentaries on Group Technology. Indeed, there tends to be a degree of overlap between Group Technology systems with highly variable demand and Flexible Cellular systems with regular repeat orders, in spite of the differences in philosophical rationale between the two types of system.

In many respects, the implementation of Flexible Manufacturing Systems has echoed earlier experience of Group Technology:

> *It is interesting that Warnecke et al. (1992) comment on the twelve years of experience in Flexible Manufacturing Systems. As has been observed, System 24, developed by Williamson and his co-workers at the Molins company, preceded this by a further twelve years, vying with Sunstrand Automation for the title of the world's first Flexible Manufacturing System. Warnecke et al. express surprise that there are few turnkey FMS installations and that the majority of the most successful ones have required radical modification with significant levels of customer involvement. Warnecke et al. emphasise the importance of the degree of attention given to the social aspects of the introduction of Advanced Manufacturing Technology as a key indicator of its potential success.*

(From Brandon 1994)

One important point to recognise is that, although both Flexible Manufacturing Systems and Group Technology are both largely insensitive to batch size, albeit for differerent reasons, the FMS will almost always cost more per component - providing G T is viable - because flexibility does not come without its costs. Williamson (1968) compared the economics of five-axis and three-axis machining centres, noting an order of magnitude difference in specific cost because of the much faster machining rate of the simpler machine.

References

J A Brandon, 1994, The anachronistic factory revisited, International Journal of Advanced Manufacturing Technology, 9, 263-270.

J Browne, D Dubois, K Rathmill, S Sethi and K Stecke, 1985, Classification of Flexible Manufacturing Systems, *in* V Bignell et al. (Editors), Manufacturing Systems: Context, Applications and Techniques, Open University/ Blackwell, Oxford.

B W Small, 1983, Wealth generation - our essential task, Proceedings of the Institution of Mechanical Engineers, **197B,** 131-141.

H Tempelmeier, 1992, Design of machining systems, *in* A Kusiak (Editor), Intelligent design and manufacturing, John Wiley, New York, 303-325.

H-J Warnecke, R Steinhilper and H Storn, 1992, A Message from the 100 FMS-Projects for Industry, 29th International Machine Tool Design and Research Conference, UMIST, Manchester, England, 213-223.

D T N Williamson, 1968, The pattern of batch manufacture and its influence on machine tool design, Proceedings of the Institution of Mechanical Engineers, **182**(1), 870-895.

INTEGRATING CELLULAR MANUFACTURING AND CORPORATE PLANNING

As has been remarked, the simplest decision aids are usually the best. This is particularly true when strategic decisions are taken that affect the structure of manufacturing systems. In these circumstances, decision-making strategies must be designed for maximum consensus and minimum managerial effort, in particular leaving no opportunity for subversion. This is only achievable if they are simple, unambiguous and robust.

One commonly used strategy in these circumstances is portfolio analysis (Hill 1983). This seeks to classify products into four simple categories according to perceptions about their current and future profitability. These are plotted on a grid according to their current market share and expected growth of the market. Of the four categories, only **cash cows** are guaranteed money-makers. With high market share but low growth potential, these are the products that generate the cash flow to develop the business. The **stars** may or may not be profitable, but this income cannot, in general, be taken out of the business; a substantial proportion of their high revenues must be committed to attaining the potential for high market growth.

market share Growth potential	Low	High
Low	pets	cash cow
High	dilemma	star

142

In the manufacturing portfolio of any mature company there will be a number of **pets** and **dilemmas**, i.e. products with unknown, or perhaps more accurately unquantified, potential but limited profitability. The pets may well be protected by a manager who sees competitive value, however misguidedly or ephemerally, in retaining these ranges in production. The dilemmas are products which through either short-sightedness or neglect have been deprived of the (perhaps minimal) investment and/or managerial commitment required to turn them into **stars**. Unfortunately, this will be exactly the justification offered by the guardians of the pets for their continued survival. The power of this advocacy should neither be underestimated nor under-rated: Alfred Sloan devoted a chapter of his autobiography to a case study of a product which brought General Motors to its knees (Chapter 5: The "copper-cooled" engine, pp.71-94 *in* Sloan 1963). The whole structure is dependent on the income from the **cash cows** whose future is far from secure.

Foster (1986) described the life cycle of a product in terms of the S-curve. As has been noted previously (Brandon 1992), similar models had long been available. The approximate positions of the categories of portfolio analysis are shown on the diagram. For the pets, no amount of additional effort will add value; the cash cows have reached the stage in their life cycle where further development effort will be beset by diminishing returns; the stars have received considerable attention and have reached the stage where they will contribute strongly to the cash flow of the enterprise; the dilemmas require additional investment of time and money before they will provide positive cash flow.

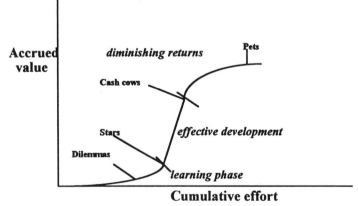

The S-curve for product development

The healthy enterprise will generate cycles of product development which exploit the different stages of maturity of their product ranges. Today's cash cows *pump-prime* the dilemmas, in the expectation that they will become tomorrow's stars, eventually to evolve into cash cows in the long term:

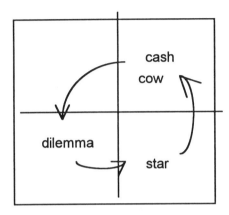

Successive cycles of product development

As has been remarked, Foster's S-curve may well have been original, but such techniques certainly were not new. However, Foster highlighted the existence of multiple S-curves for each product. Although further evolutionary improvements to a product or process may not be worthwhile, there might be considerable potential in examining more radical innovations. Maybe new manufacturing processes are available that were unavailable or otherwise inappropriate when the product was developed; perhaps new markets can be developed for mature products. This is just the context where value analysis is most appropriate (Miles 1961,Gage 1967).

Assuming that value analysis has been carried out, and that product strategies have been developed throughout the range, there are certain general rules that can be developed to implement cellular manufacturing:

Cash cows:

- These are products which have been made for some time;

144

- They are likely to be made on traditional machines in process-based production;
- Their useful life is probably limited;
- Their volume is large - what Parnaby (1981) decribes as **runners** - such as to be the financial mainstay of the organisation.

Likely solution:

Group technology flowlines

High volume justifies specialising the tooling and layout, linked to materials handling, even within the cell;

Using existing machines in a Group Technology system permits their recovery at the end of the product cycle.

Dilemmas:

- These are products whose future requirements are currently unknown;
- They are likely to be made on traditional machines in process-based production;
- As yet, the amount of useful data for system design is limited;
- Their volume is small - what Parnaby (1981) decribes as **strangers** - such as to be largely irrelevant to the financial wellbeing of the organisation.

Likely solution:

Flexible manufacturing cells

There is not yet enough confidence in the product's future to customise the cell layout for materials handling, i.e. not a flowline;

It is expected that production plant suitable for assembling Group Technology cells will be released as the cash cows move into obsolescence - assuming the product meets its expectations.

Stars:

- These are products which have been made for some time;
- They are likely to be made on traditional machines in process-based production;
- There is confidence that these will be made in volume;
- Their volume is currently relatively low - what Parnaby (1981) decribes as **repeaters** - but is predicted to rise.

Likely solution:

Group technology cells

Uncertainty about future demand mix suggests that design of flowlines is premature - although it is the long- term solution if expectations are realised.

Pets:

- These are products which have been made for some time;
- They are likely to be made on traditional machines in process-based production;
- Their useful life is probably limited;
- Their continued presence in the range can only be justified on the basis of a strategic decision;
- Their volume is likely to be highly variable but quite small.

Likely solution:

Flexible manufacturing cells

Rational analysis suggests that these products should simply be deleted from the range, but they may be sleeping dilemmas - the essence of an FMS is that there is no additional cost in maintaining products in the range for strategic purposes.

References

J A Brandon, 1992, Structural impediments to strategic change in the technological enterprise, Journal of Strategic Change, 1(6), 333-339.

R N Foster, 1986, Innovation: the Attacker's advantage, Macmillan, London.

W L Gage, 1967, Value Analysis, McGraw-Hill, London.

T J Hill, 1983, Production and Operations Management, Prentice-Hall, London.

L D Miles, 1961, Techniques of Value Analysis and Engineering, McGraw-Hill, New York.

J Parnaby, 1981, Concept of a Manufacturing System, *in* Systems Behaviour, 3rd Edn, Paul Chapman/Open University, 131-141. (Also International Journal of Production Research, 17(2), 1979.)

A P Sloan Jr., 1963, My years with General Motors, Sidgwick and Jackson, London.

FUTURE MANUFACTURING SYSTEMS

For reasons which will be explained, it can reasonably be expected that **all future manufacturing systems will be organised along cellular principles**. Thus the key problem is how this can be implemented in the most effective manner.

The 1980s were characterised by **Islands of automation.** Companies had achieved sophisticated automation locally, robots, numerically controlled machines, etc., but could not yet integrate these units into automated manufacturing systems. Roger Smith , the Chairman of General Motors in 1984, likened the state of automation in his company to a *Tower of Babel* with typically only fifteen percent. of programmable devices able to communicate outside their processes (Anon. 1985).

The preoccupation of technologists in the 1980s was the linking of the Islands of Automation (Cameron 1987). Although the basic concepts were established by Williamson (1968) some twenty years earlier, and despite unprecedented reserves of computer power, this vision has yet to be realised. The pace of change in technology has defeated the attempts to standardise communications systems. Once again, it must be emphasised that this will only occur when a general consensus prevails that new technologies must be constrained to enable standardisation (Brandon 1994).

It is a fundamental premise of this work that, if manufacturing systems are to be coordinated in the form desired by Roger Smith, the managerial infrastructure must be compatible with the technology (Skinner 1971). This can only be so if the structure of the technology can be represented in a form that is accessible to decision makers. Thus the acceptance of new technologies is dependent on the visualisation of its essential concepts in a simple imagery.

Imagery of structural modelling

Influential management authors have developed ideas to describe the structure of organisations and change, which have been articulated in simple and colourful imagery (Kanter 1989, Peters 1992, Hammer and Champy 1993, Naisbitt 1993). In *The New Realities* (1989), Peter Drucker returned to his earlier contention that the British Raj - flat hierarchy with total empowerment, the Symphony Orchestra - symbiotic specialisms, and the Teaching Hospital - co-existent functional specialists working independently to a common corporate goal, were suitable models for the organisation of the future (see also Drucker 1992). Latterly Drucker has projected an image of the knowledge society as a *knowledge flotilla*. This suggests a consensus of corporate vision that Peters (1989) suggests is contradicted by survey evidence in many companies. Developing from the islands of automation, it has been suggested that the *knowledge archipelago* is a more neutral term (Brandon 1993). Skinner's analysis suggests that technological change will only take place if affinities can be demonstrated between these trends in corporate design and the infrastructure requirements of the technology.

The model of the future suggested by Deal and Kennedy (1982) is typical. They describe the *Organization of the Future* in the following terms:

- *small task-focused work units (ten to twenty persons maximum),*
- *each with economic and management control over its own destiny,*
- *interconnected with larger entities through benign computer and communication links,*
- *and bonded into larger companies through strong cultural bonds.*

To satisfy Skinner's (!971) criteria, one must be able to recognise compatible ideas and methodologies in the technological literature. Perhaps most influential of these has been the writing of Hans-Jürgen Warnecke, President of the Fraunhofer Society. Warnecke's solution is the *Fractal Company* (1993). Warnecke visualises future manufacturing systems to be based on fractals, complex organisational units which have the essential feature of self-similarity - the key to their management. An alternative, yet compatible, view expressed here is modelling manufacturing systems using ideas from *object-oriented programming systems* (OOPS).

To automate or not to automate: that is the question..

The two types of cellular manufacturing presented here differ fundamentally in their approach to automation. This is best appreciated in the context of A P Alford's third law of Scientific Management (Alford 1940): that Flexible Manufacturing Systems inherently transfer skill to the machine whereas Group Technology, as originally envisaged, transfers skill to the workers (Brandon 1992).

There is a growing tendency in the literature on manufacturing management to reject high-technology solutions. This is based partially on the perceived track record of Advanced Manufacturing Technology, which is seen as promising too much and delivering too little and usually late. The second reason is the recognition that high technology disrupts the social order of the enterprise. In keeping with Skinner's analysis, both effects are reinforced by inappropriate corporate infrastructure.

Particularly influential in the movement to reject unnecessary automation has been Richard Schonberger (1987a,b,1990). He contends that automated systems *disconnect people, obscure opportunities ... and result in divided accountability.* This echoed Williamson's (1968) analysis some twenty years earlier.

Recent developments in computational methodology have made the question superfluous in the sense argued by Schonberger. It has become possible to introduce sophisticated automated systems which remain under the local control of the shopfloor.

An Object-Oriented World

There could be no better demonstration of Skinner's criteria for change than the technology of object-oriented programming systems (OOPS). Widely viewed as a recent development, the key ideas of OOPS were actually implemented in the early 1960s in the Smalltalk language (Goldberg and Robson 1983). There is no doubt that their applicability was inhibited technologically: computers were simply not powerful enough to exploit the technology to the full - the same could be said of numerical control. What was more of an inhibition was the received view that computing was the preserve of large centralised data-processing departments who functionalised their workload into monolithic programmes. If this is Tuesday, this must be the payroll!

OOPS are best understood by comparison with traditional programming systems. A traditional procedural programme would be constructed and stored on magnetic tape. When data processing was undertaken, this programme would be loaded into memory and would operate on a data file stored on a different magnetic tape. The result of the computer run would be output onto a third magnetic tape.

The object-oriented system works quite differently. The key feature is that the separation between procedures and data is eliminated: both are *encapsulated* within an *object*. Communication between objects is achieved by *message passing*. The state of the object is changed according to its *methods*. New objects may be constructed from existing ones by a process of *inheritance*, making system design efficient and effective. The properties of objects may be generalised into *classes* which are themselves objects. A member of a class is called an *instance*. System constraints may be imposed on an object by means of an embedded method known as a *demon*.

Consider an analogous problem in production management. In traditional functional organisations an operative would receive a job card for assembly of a batch of products. This would initiate a tour of the factory: to the materials stores for components; to the drawing store for assembly instructions; to the tool store for appropriate tools; etc. (usually with a great deal of etcetera). In the alternative - object oriented - factory, the batch of products is provided to the operative as a *kit*. Together with the components are delivered the assembly drawings and all tools and consumables necessary for completing the batch.

What constitutes an object is extremely general - any non-trivial entity which participates in the manufacturing system: products, processes, machinery, personnel, etc.

Object-oriented programming systems are now widely used in the modelling of manufacturing systems (Brandon et al. 1995). Their compatibility with manufacturing systems is treated at greater length in Brandon (1993). They form the basis of more sophisticated anthropomorphic systems, with capabilities for conflict resolution, negotiation, explanation, etc., described as *Agents* (Huang and Brandon 1993).

The object-oriented factory

Manufacturing systems, in their traditional context, entail only the processes of material transformation. Using the object-oriented system methodology allows this to be treated much more generally. In this manner true factories-within-factories, with all of the range of functional activities, can be realised. Amongst accountants, for example, *Activity-Based Costing* is eminently suitable for an object-oriented approach (Innes et al. 1994). A general accounting object can be inherited into a cell and adapted to fulfil an extremely specialised role within the cell. A choice of production-control objects can be incorporated, dependent on whether its principal role is in processing runners (KANBAN), repeaters (MRP), or strangers (MRPII) (Parnaby et al. 1987).

Because the principal external interface of object-oriented systems is specifically tailored to communication, members of the cell can use the systems without relinquishing their autonomy, particularly where the more general agent-based approach is used.

References

L P Alford, 1940, Principles of Industrial Management, The Ronald Press, New York.
Anon., 1985 (June), Communications-Friendly Machines are Needed on our Factory Floors, Mechanical Engineering, 34-39.
J A Brandon, 1992, Managing Change in Manufacturing Systems, Productivity Publishing, Olney, England.
J A Brandon, 1993, From the islands of automation to the knowledge archipelago: the challenge for manufacturing strategy in the 1990s, Proceedings of the Institution of Mechanical Engineers - Journal of Engineering Manufacture, **B207**, 141-146.
J A Brandon, 1994, The anachronistic factory revisited, International Journal of Advanced Manufacturing Technology, 9, 263-270.
J A Brandon, M Troll and E Vollmer, 1995, From distributed production control to disseminated production management, Fifth International Conference on Flexible

152

Automation and Intelligent Manufacturing, Stuttgart, Editors, R D Schraft et al., 393-403.

G R Cameron, 1987, From Islands of Automation to Integrated CAE, Computers in Mechanical Engineering, 14-19.

T. Deal and A. Kennedy, 1982, Corporate Cultures: The Rites and Rituals of Corporate Life, Addison-Wesley, New York.

P F Drucker, 1989, The New Realities, Butterworth-Heinemann, Oxford, England.

P F Drucker, 1992, Managing for the Future, Butterworth-Heinemann, Oxford, England.

A Goldberg and D Robson, Smalltalk-80: the language and its implementation, Addison-Wesley, New York.

M Hammer and J Champy, 1993, Reengineering the corporation: A manifesto for business revolution, Nicholas Brearley, London.

G Q Huang and J A Brandon, 1993, Cooperating Expert Systems in Mechanical Design, Research Studies Press, Taunton, England.

J Innes, F Mitchell and T Yoshikawa, 1994, Activity Based Costing for Engineers, Research Studies Press, Taunton/ John Wiley, Chichester.

R M Kanter, 1989, When giants learn to dance: Mastering the challenge of Strategy, Management and Careers in the 1990s, Simon and Schuster, London.

J Naisbitt, 1993, Global Paradox: The bigger the world economy the more powerful its smallest players, Nicholas Brearley, London

J Parnaby, P Johnson and B Herbison, 1987, Development of the JIT-MRP factory control system, Second International Conference on Computer-Aided Production Engineering, Edinburgh, Mechanical Engineering Publications, Bury St Edmunds, 17-22.

T Peters, 1989, Thriving on Chaos: Handbook for a Management Revolution, Macmillan, London.

T Peters, 1992, Liberation Management: Necessary Disorganisation for the Nanosecond Nineties, Pan Macmillan, London.

R. J. Schonberger, 1987a (September-October), Frugal Manufacturing, Harvard Business Review, 95-100.

R. J. Schonberger, 1987b, World Class Manufacturing Casebook: Implementing JIT and TQC, The Free Press, New York.

R. J. Schonberger, 1990, Building a Chain of Customers: Linking Business Functions to Create the World Class Company, Hutchinson Business Books, London.

W Skinner, 1971 (January - February), The Anachronistic Factory, Harvard Business Review, 61-70.

H J Warnecke, 1993, The Fractal Company: A Revolution in Corporate Culture, Springer-Verlag, Berlin (published previously in 1992 as *Die Fraktale Fabrik)*.

D T N Williamson, 1968, The pattern of batch manufacture and its influence on machine tool design, Proceedings of the Institution of Mechanical Engineers, **182**, 870-895.

EPILOGUE

The reader looking for prescriptive solutions to the implementation of Cellular Manufacturing Systems will doubtless be disappointed by this book. However, it is **essential** to recognise that **there are no general prescriptions** for this problem. The book is not so much a **how to do it** text as a **how others failed to do it properly** report. There are many such experiences, but it takes a determined investigator to find them. Companies are always willing to publicise their successes - but rather more reluctant to admit their failures in public.

As has been suggested, Cellular Manufacturing Systems are likely to be the default organisation in the factory of the future. Cellular Manufacturing should be seen in its broadest context, however:

> *The use of the term "cell" should not be seen to exclude non-manufacturing groups, for example the linking of workstations in a design office. Indeed, as remarked by Horvath [1988], there is no consensus as to a unique definition of what constitutes a cell.*

> (Brandon 1993)

The text has used the expression **factory-within-a-factory** to describe the necessity for involvement of staff outside the traditional production disciplines in cellular manufacturing. The manufacturing organisation of the future will more probably comprise **businesses-within-businesses,** with all of the existing functions of the enterprise devolved to the product level. This is achievable through object-oriented

156

programming methodologies, based on local production control, activity-based costing, and other micro-disciplines.

The technological minimalists, like Schonberger (1987a,b,1990), advocate ripping out unnecessary transfer technology on the basis that it disrupts natural communication between the staff in manufacturing. He is quite correct - but the key word is *unnecessary*. As has been described, Toyota have now developed transfer-line management techniques which continue to respect the intelligence of the worker. If these arguments are taken to their logical conclusion, however, shopfloor workers must be given the option of introducing automation to assist their work. The priorities of the technological minimalists can be reconciled with the views of automation technologists by recourse to the object-oriented methodology.

The widespread inability to complete the process of integration of manufacturing systems has been attributed to a fundamental structural defect of the traditionally organised manufacturing enterprise (Brandon 1992a). In particular, the four prerequisites of change: authority, resources, expertise and motivation, may be separated, the first two retained by corporate centre which may not have the technical capability to define appropriate strategies for change (Brandon 1992b).

If there is one issue that unites all commentators it is that investment in people is the surest way to success in implementing cellular manufacturing. For example, Ingersoll Engineers (1990) found dramatic evidence of the correlation between successful implementation and investment in people and management systems:

Comparative investment	All companies	Top ten percent.
People	18%	43%
Buildings and environment	14%	0%
Management and Control systems	24%	29%
Equipment, materials handling and tooling	23%	14%
Machines and processes	21%	14%

(abstracted from Figure 15c of Ingersoll 1990)

Thus the investment in people is paramount. Their **empowerment** (a popular word in the management literature but used very sparingly here) has three aspects:

Staff are not only authorised, but are actually required, to take whatever decisions they can (subject to satisfying the mission of the enterprise and testing their own competence) without seeking external approval.

Staff are charged with appraisal of their own competence and with seeking out, and acquiring, specialist knowledge that is perceived as an inhibition on their performance of their duties.

Staff have a general duty to enhance the performance of their individual colleagues and work groups, which must include increasing their knowledge. However, in the interests of both efficiency and effectiveness, such mutual support must be subject to personal envelopes of influence; otherwise too many staff are likely to be spending too much time and energy seeking out and remedying the deficiencies of others. After all, there is no point in devising the perfect manufacturing organisation if nobody is actually making any saleable product.

(Brandon 1993).

References

J A Brandon, 1992a, Structural impediments to strategic change in the technological enterprise, Journal of Strategic Change, 1(6), 333-339.

J A Brandon, 1992, Managing Change in Manufacturing Systems, Productivity Publishing, Olney, England.

J A Brandon, 1993, From the islands of automation to the knowledge archipelago: the challenge for manufacturing strategy in the 1990s, Proceedings of the Institution of Mechanical Engineers - Journal of Engineering Manufacture, **B207**, 141-146.

M Horvath, 1988, Manufacturing Engineering: The Birth and Growth of a New Science, Robotics and Computer Integrated Manufacturing, 4(1/2), 285-292.

Ingersoll Engineers, 1990, Competitive Manufacturing: The Quiet Revolution, Ingersoll Engineers, Rugby, England.

158

R. J. Schonberger, 1987a (September-October), Frugal Manufacturing, Harvard Business Review, 95-100.

R. J. Schonberger, 1987b, World Class Manufacturing Casebook: Implementing JIT and TQC, The Free Press, New York.

R. J. Schonberger, 1990, Building a Chain of Customers: Linking Business Functions to Create the World Class Company, Hutchinson Business Books, London.

INDEX

Coventry University